The Statues Gasped

A book of hope about learning to trust in God to come to a place of healing and freedom, written by a survivor and a chaplain.

Sarah J Chapman
&
Anna

First published 2020

ISBN: PB: 978-1-83853-280-2; ebook: 978-1-83853-281-9

A CIP record for this book is available from the British Library.

Edited by Helen Jones
Cover Design by Eliana Thompson

Dedication

This book is dedicated to all survivors of abuse travelling on their own journey… those we have been blessed to encounter and those not known to us.

Acknowledgements

We would like to thank the many people who encouraged and inspired us, particularly when it felt too hard to complete: Ruth Chapman, Anne Davidson, Steve Gendall, Clare Gibson, Nick Papadopulos and Richard Wyld. In particular our editor Helen Jones, our designer, Eliana Thompson and our administrator Giles Chapman whose care for us both was, and is, amazing. We give thanks to everyone who faithfully prayed for us, both on the healing journey itself and in the creation of this book.

Sarah gives particular thanks 'to all the people who have trusted me with their life stories and their prayers for me. This book would never have been written without you. The shared journey of healing has been inspirational and awesome. Thank you for allowing me to be a part of it.'

Anna gives thanks 'to every single person who believed me and supported me on my journey since I was a young child. Each in their own way gave me hope and courage to keep going. You all individually and collectively held a light in my darkness. Thank you.'

Contents

Introduction

This is a book about hope and love and mystery. Anna had experienced abuse throughout her childhood by her parents and never spoke about the abuse until she was an adult. She had spent many years in therapy where she found partial recovery from the trauma. However, through a developing faith in Jesus she found that the pain of abuse within her began to heal in ways she never imagined.

Sarah and Anna write about that healing pilgrimage from both perspectives – Sarah as a chaplain facilitating the healing, and Anna as a survivor of childhood abuse. The book shares Anna's journey as an internal pilgrimage of faith and recovery from trauma, as well as a physical pilgrimage of worship at Canterbury Cathedral during that time.

The healing journey describes how Anna's developing faith in God began to untangle her own identity. Anna understood the truth of her identity as a loved child of God rather than the lies about her identity that had been created within her during the abuse. Finding the truth of who she was in God enabled Anna to understand herself and her trauma in new ways. She shares the reality of living daily with the pain of abuse, but over time as she trusted in God she began to let go of the memories and pain in ways she had never been able to do previously. This was only possible once Anna learnt to love and care for herself, every part of her traumatised self, with the help of Sarah. And once she was able to let Jesus into that pain within her, the healing began to transform. The journey was not easy and there were times of deep sadness and loss. But as she walked on with Jesus she began to find a new emotional and spiritual freedom. It was transforming on many levels and her whole life changed as a result. Anna shares, 'This book is about the hope which I found. My journey won't be the same as anyone else's journey and this book isn't a self-help guide to freedom from abuse. But it is a book of hope, about learning to trust in God to come to a place of healing and freedom.'

Sarah reflects on her wider experiences of supporting and ministering to those who have suffered abuse and trauma, both outside the church and from within the church. Sarah describes the impact of trauma on people both internally and spiritually. The importance of listening well is critical to her ministry with those who have suffered abuse and she shares the importance of listening and praying with every traumatised part of the person she is with. She reveals the mystery of healing that Jesus brings and how to be alongside and support those seeking recovery from abuse. Sarah shares 'What is ultimately needed is a heart large enough to love another deeply and unconditionally, to believe that God loves you and will help you through the journey. What is also critical is to spend time with God so you remain filled up and focused on Him and to be a person of prayer – to pray for others, as well as pray and be prayed for. I know that there is real hope for survivors of abuse to heal and I want to encourage others that it is possible.'

Chapter 1
The Statues Gasped

Sarah

It was a Sunday morning at the cathedral, and I sat in the congregation. For some reason I'd decided to worship at the cathedral that day. I worshipped there occasionally but not all the time. I soon discovered why I'd felt called to be there that day. The sermon was preached by an American lady, a guest speaker and she began speaking about healing and abuse. She said the word 'sexual' several times in Canterbury Cathedral and I could almost hear the statues gasp, let alone other members of the congregation! She preached with honesty, hope and without underestimating the pain of it all, but she challenged us to actually do something. The Bible verse she used was 'Stand up, take your mat and walk' (John 5:8), the words Jesus spoke after healing an ill man. But the words 'take your mat and walk', echoed in my mind. The words were speaking to me about what God may be asking me to do in my own ministry. Most of my ministry is with those who are hurting, more on the inside from the agonising memories of the past, than anything that is visibly paralysing. The internal pain that many experience can nonetheless be emotionally paralysing.

I thought about The Living Well and how it had really become a place of prayer, where people are encouraged to get into the pool of God's love and grace. I had been working at The Living Well (The Canterbury Diocesan Centre for healing and wholeness) as a chaplain and diocesan advisor, supporting individuals, groups, parishes and clergy in the healing ministry. What I often felt I was doing with Anna and many other people was to be alongside them, bringing the healing love of Jesus, where they are helped into the water so their healing can happen. And then they are helped to 'get up and walk'. Walk into a new place of freedom and transformation. And as I was challenged by the words in this sermon, I continued wondering whether God was asking something more of me in all this. I think He was. The healing days that were offered at The Living Well, and that take place around the diocese, offer an opportunity for anyone to engage in the living, healing God. What I had seen on those days is that things shift for people, changes happen, and people are healed in extraordinary ways. God's work is miraculous and continues to be a mystery.

I was sitting next to Anna as this sermon was preached and I thought about the healing journey she was on from suffering abuse by her parents. I thought about how I was bearing witness to her recovery from the trauma she experienced as a child and how I was almost standing to one side, watching and waiting as He brought her to the next step. I pondered all this some more with God and thought about the church and if the church offers this opportunity. I am finding that I am supporting an ever-increasing number of adults who have suffered abuse, including abuse within the church. There is a real issue about what members and leaders of the church have done when they have been perpetrators of abuse, when they have been part of that abuse, when they have sexually abused, when they have sexually attached themselves to those in their care or committed any type of abuse. At such times it is as if the very place that should be a place of healing and safety has instead become a place of darkness, sickness and evil. This is true, in part, when the church has badly managed those who have been abused by other members of the church, and has worked hard to rescue the perpetrators to hide and keep the abuse 'secret'. It is also true when the church has not helped or cared for victims in any way. As a priest, I feel ashamed of how the church has behaved and know that we can't make it all right again by saying sorry. We can never make it alright for the person who has suffered; what they have suffered is appalling and can never be made right. We may, with God's grace, some time and space, and with really open listening, enable some survivors to move on and not be defined by the trauma of the abuse they have suffered at 'our hands'.

There is something we can do in an active way and I have done so when leading services for survivors of abuse. In the Bible we find the story of Daniel praying what is sometimes called a prayer of representational confession (Daniel 9:3–19). Daniel has done nothing wrong himself, but nevertheless he asks, even begs, God for forgiveness, on behalf of the people of God. Daniel stands in the gap and takes on the wrongdoings of others but says the prayer from a personal place, owning the wrongdoing. The church would do well to lament and repent of the way we have behaved towards the children of God. We as church members can do the same and ask God's forgiveness for what has happened. This is what I have found myself doing when leading worship at specific services for survivors of abuse. (Appendix 1)

As with all abuse there is a fundamental fear, 'Who will believe me?' Many victims are told that the abuse was 'a secret'. And people think that this person of authority, this vicar, this family member, this person of high standing in a community could not possibly have done this. And the victim thinks that no one would believe that the abuse happened in a church, or church setting. We have seen in recent years that those who have easy access to children (such as football coaches, famous personalities, teachers and more) open the door to those who choose to be predators to abuse. The church also has a history of enabling such access and the consequent appalling stories of those who have been abused while in the care of the church have been hitting the headlines for some time. Clergy and church leaders are in the position of power but within a faith there is also the place of spiritual authority. This, as with any position of authority, can become tainted and misused.

Kneeling to receive the sacrament of communion means that you are at eye level of the person's genitals. How does that feel if that person has been abusing you in the vestry the previous day? It becomes an impossible situation to understand, to accept and to move through. Where is God in all this if God's representative is 'allowed' to do this, telling the victim all the while that it is for 'their own good', part of the sacrifice to make them a better person or to bring them closer to experiencing the love of God? The lies go on and on and it then becomes incredibly difficult for the victim, often a child, to distinguish the truth from the lie. In the confusion of the appalling level of lying, victims are left doubting how they can find the true God and who He is?

The abuse may well be physical and sexual, but it can also be spiritual. Members and leaders in the church who have been unable to sit with and experience the pain of a person's disclosure being expressed, because they find it so painful, may end up denying the narrative. When what 'I' think or 'I' feel becomes more important than the victim and their need, there is no safe space and no real heart listening. The abused person can then quite rightly and understandably feel re-traumatised. The spiritual denial can take the form of prayer over the person to 'rid them of this demon of lust' or to remove the 'spirit of lies' or to insist they need to forgive the perpetrator. This perpetuates the abuse for victims and, in my experience, stifles the healing.

I feel the enormity of this pain in my work in the church. But I believe and know it is possible to still have a faith even when those in authority in the faith have perpetuated the abuse. It is only possible if there is a willingness to listen, to take lots of time to tease out what was the lie... and what is the truth. Just because this person held a position of authority and had a degree in theology it does not mean that how they expressed their faith was OK. A survivor needs to know, and believe, it was not OK; it was very wrong.

In someone coming alongside and listening, and in the discovery of the difference between the truth and the lies, the survivor experiences the touch of healing, the breath of the Holy Spirit bringing life and freedom. In many ways it might be seen as a reformation moment, like that moment when the church reformer, Martin Luther (1483–1546), got back to the truth of what the gospels were saying. We cannot buy God's love or His overwhelming grace. The truth of who God is becomes real, and then the false image of God that has been shared and taught as part of the abuse can be seen for what it is, and placed at the foot of the cross along with the memories and pain. This will take time; healing does take time, as with a broken bone that needs time to mend and heal.

It was all of this, and my increased ministry with those in pain from abuse, whether from within the church or a completely different setting, that challenged me after listening to the sermon. I felt challenged to continue providing that place for people to walk into the pool of God's healing, to get up, pick up their mat and walk into a new place of freedom. I have walked alongside Anna in her experience of just that, which is shared with you in this book. But I also share my experiences of walking with many people who seek to be freed from the chains of abuse.

Anna

When I first met Sarah, I was only just beginning to explore my faith in God. I wasn't even sure I knew what it would mean to be healed or even whether I could be healed. I had suffered abuse as a child in various forms; sexually, physically and emotionally by the very people entrusted with my care – my parents. The experience of suffering abuse as a child meant that inside me my heart was broken time and time again. I had never spoken about the abuse until I reached adulthood and left home, but the effects had left me desperately unhappy, lonely, fearful, confused, depressed and at times suicidal. I had always been determined to find a way to recover and I spent most of my adult life in and out of therapy trying to find an inner resolution for myself. Therapy helped me enormously. It helped me to have a much deeper understanding of myself and to gain an ability to start trusting others. I also think it helped me to develop a stronger sense of myself, to understand my own relational being and gain an ability to trust in the process rather than dictate it. However, despite all this, there was something that never healed for me in therapy. It continued to cause immense pain deep inside me. It never healed my heart. Despite all the therapy, I continued to have this deep-seated pain and yearning to feel loved and cared for. The pain in my heart from being broken each time I was abused remained and I had feared it would never be healed.

As I sat next to Sarah listening to the sermon at Canterbury Cathedral, at first I was shocked that someone had dared to talk about abuse in a service! But then it made me think about how over the past couple of years the pain in my heart had been healing. I don't say this lightly, but it happened through my developing faith in God. I didn't walk into my faith with rose-tinted glasses; I was initially skeptical and doubted. So, I empathise with anyone who is skeptical about my testimony. However, I know that through my faith, it had been the love of Jesus that truly healed my heart, healed my pain and freed me. When the preacher spoke about the words 'take up your mat and walk', I thought about how hard that had been at times. It certainly hadn't been easy, and it hadn't been pain free. My whole life changed as a result, but I now bear witness to the mystery and healing power of Jesus and know that recovery from the pain of abuse is absolutely possible.

I thought about what my own expectations of healing had been on the journey. What do we expect from healing? What do we believe will happen when we are healed? What are we expecting of Jesus in our healing?

I thought about this a lot and often read many articles about people's frustrations of feeling they had not been healed from long-term illnesses, enduring mental health conditions or trauma. It has made me think about the gospel teachings and observations of healing. The stories are miraculous, often written as a quick demonstration of a touch of Jesus that brings sight to the blind, hearing to the deaf, cleansing of skin or medical conditions, ability for the paralysed to walk and raising of the dead. In the Bible Jesus often used short sharp commands to people when he healed them, for example; 'get up', 'pick up your mat and go', 'go and tell', 'don't tell anyone'; and sends people on their way – a new way.

When I think about my own healing journey from suffering abuse, I know that my healing started with having faith in Jesus. The important point is that my healing did not eradicate the abuse I'd suffered; it was part of my life, something I'll always live with in my human life. But through my faith in Jesus I was healed from the chains of pain and fear that the abuse had wrapped me in. My healing gave me freedom; to get up, walk, see and live my life in Christ. It freed me from shame and guilt – all the feelings that did not belong to me. The memories of abuse are still with me; sometimes I think about it and sometimes it upsets me. But the difference I feel, in being healed from it, is that each time I go through the pain I know Jesus understands because he went through the pain of the cross. And he knows what it is like to long for the pain to ease. There is light even within the darkness of the tomb because Jesus is there with me.

Being healed through having faith did at times feel miraculous. It's hard to describe or explain but I sometimes experienced it most powerfully as I sat in the cathedral. Throughout my healing I worshipped at Canterbury Cathedral regularly. It was the most wonderful space to sit in and just be, especially in times of excruciating emotional pain. It was as if the building and all it had held spiritually over the centuries could just hold me. I felt held by God in that space, wherever I sat, and whichever chapel I found myself worshipping in.

I remembered one particular evening at evensong, which was one of my favourite services to attend. There is something about the music, the rhythm of prayer and scriptures which I find so beautiful. Whether I'm sad, in pain, exhausted, happy or anxious, the rhythm of evensong takes me on a 45-minute journey of its own. So, on this particular day I sat listening to the scriptures. The Dean was reading a gospel passage and I was reminded of my grandfather who was the only adult that had ever read to me as a child. He didn't read me a bedtime story often, but his stories were such fun. As a young child, I had hated bedtimes and had been extremely fearful of going to bed and going to sleep. But when my grandad cared for me on the occasional evening, he used to make up stories, full of imagination, and it was the most wonderful thing to experience as a child who spent much of her time afraid and confused. He gave me the gift of freedom in those stories as a child – freedom, for a time, from the pain of abuse.

As I sat listening to the gospel reading that evening, it struck me how important it was in my healing to sit and listen to the scriptures, listen in wonder and anticipation as I had with my grandfather. But the words I was listening to now were God's. They weren't just about imagination, they were about reality – a reality of how God could set me free, completely free, not just temporarily.

The Dean continued reading the passage and as I thought about the significance of hearing the scriptures being read to me, I then had such a powerful feeling. 'This is where I have found true love' I said in my head. Being in the cathedral had begun to feel like home for me. It had become my spiritual home, the place where I could turn up and be with my Heavenly Father. That in itself had been healing. I had grown up abused by my earthly father. In this journey of healing, through my faith, I had somehow learnt to trust in God as my Father. So, sitting at evensong on that particular day, the feeling that came which said, 'this is where I have found true love', was incredible. God had helped me to know what it is like to feel 'at home' and to feel 'loved'. These were two feelings I had never experienced before but had been longing for.

As I thought about these moments of healing, and listened to the sermon with Sarah that morning, it really helped me to understand Jesus' words he often said: 'Your faith has made you well'. Healing can't take away memories, loss, physical or mental health conditions. But living with our humanness and fragility, in the love of Christ, he heals us from the chains of those things that can hold us in and cause immense pain.

Chapter 2
Faith

Sarah

In this chapter Anna talks about her faith and how that helped her to understand herself as the child of God that I always believed her to be.

Anna

Finding God and then learning the truth about God were both very significant elements in the initial part of my healing. I share with you a little about my journey into faith.

As a child I grew up attending church regularly, but I never truly believed in God. In fact, during services I would never say the words aloud during worship and only mouthed them so no one would notice I wasn't speaking. I never understood how there could be a God when I was being hurt so badly. It didn't make sense to me and I therefore remained doubtful. I always wondered if there was a God, but I didn't believe God could help me in my life. As a child being hurt repeatedly, it didn't make sense how God could be there and not help me.

However, later on in life, a couple of years before I met Sarah at The Living Well, my auntie was dying of cancer. She was a lady so strong in faith, and I saw it most poignantly in the last two months of her life as her health deteriorated rapidly. She was so unafraid of death and in her words, she was 'waiting for the Lord', almost impatiently. 'When will he take me?' she used to ask me over and over again. I found it astonishing that her faith was her absolute strength at that time. Looking back, I think in my auntie's longing to meet the Lord, his presence also reached me. I felt the closest I had ever felt to my auntie in the last two months of her life and it was such a blessing. I'm ever thankful to my auntie for showing me her faith so clearly.

When I visited my auntie during that time, a priest who had provided support to her was often there. I began to talk to the priest and then made contact with her away from my auntie and I told her about the abuse. It had been the first time I had ever told anyone within the church about the abuse I'd suffered within my family. The priest was incredibly supportive and was the first person who ever sat and prayed with me alone. I immediately felt the power of prayer which I'd never experienced before. Each time she prayed with me, I started crying – the tears and emotion almost coming from nowhere.

In one of the conversations the priest said to me 'the truth will set you free'. Those six words stuck in my mind like glue and I repeated them over and over in my head after that visit. It was as if something inside me suddenly heard the hope of freedom. 'Could I really be free?' I questioned in my head. I held on to those six words.

Something about the words initially spurred me on to have the courage and bravery in therapy to talk about all the abuse, some of which I'd never spoken about before. The next couple of years of therapy were spent working tirelessly through that and uncovering what had never been uncovered. It was an extremely painful process and very tiring.

Following my auntie's death and having further discussions with the priest, I became more and more interested in my faith. I started reading things about God and thinking about my faith. I also made contact with an organisation called Life Centre[a]. It was the only organisation I had known that combined recovery from sexual abuse with faith. Discussing faith was an optional part of the service they offered and not a requirement for those coming along. But I did want to discuss my faith. The conversations I had with them enabled me to ask questions about God in a way I'd never done before.

I then began reading the Bible. It may not seem an easy book to pick up and start reading and in fact I had never known how to even approach it! Some of it had looked impossible. I didn't even know how to navigate my way around the Bible – I knew there was an Old Testament and a New Testament and the stories about Jesus were in the New Testament and that was about it.

When I had been quite unwell over a period of a few weeks I couldn't tolerate a lot at the time and all I wanted to do was sit in bed and read. As Easter was approaching, I decided to read the Easter story. I couldn't tell you from which gospel I read it; it was just the first one I found. I knew the story, but I'd never read the story from the Bible in this way before. Over a few days I read a little bit at a time. I read about how unjustly Jesus was treated and it resonated with me. But what I also read about was how Jesus was ready and prepared to do what he had been sent to do. And I read the pain of that moment when it was darkness and he felt alone – the very real feelings we all experience as human beings.

And then, suddenly, as I read through the Easter story, it made complete sense to me what being a Christian is all about – the thing that I needed to believe in most of all was that God had given his only Son, Jesus Christ, to die on the cross and to rise from the dead; and that he did this to give us hope. In a world full of sin, by him doing this – dying and being resurrected – he had given all of us an opportunity for hope, forgiveness and eternal life. I remember so vividly lying in bed declaring my faith to God and saying aloud 'I believe'.

After having attended church for years as a child, why had this suddenly come as a surprise to me? Wasn't this something I should have known? Something I should have felt? As a child being abused at home, I had stood in church not understanding God because of my own suffering and so as a child I'd just left my faith at that point – unknowing and unbelieving. At the time I had desperately wanted to be kept safe and at the time I'd thought if God couldn't do that, no one could. So, I had rejected God and everyone else too. It was simple: if I could be alone, no one could hurt me. So, in my internal world, that was the choice I'd made. That was until the events surrounding and following my auntie's death, when I was prompted in quite extraordinary ways to reconsider my choice and reconsider my faith and beliefs.

Not many months after personally declaring my faith, I made a significant decision to surrender my life to God. It was an incredibly dark place to be in emotionally but it was at that point, lying in bed not knowing how much more pain I could take, I said aloud, 'God I give all this to you now; you lead and I'll follow'. I surrendered my life to God that day, it feeling like the only option I had, but with a deep knowing that I wanted to let God help me. My surrendering was not a 'giving up', but a decision to allow God to be at the forefront of my life. It was one of the hardest things to do when I had survived abuse by ensuring I was very much in control of my life. Some days I found it almost impossible! But every day I made my choice – do I want to go this alone or with God? Not being with God now felt the more impossible of the two!

Not long after that I found out about The Living Well and arranged to meet Sarah. I've always wondered about the timings of it. The way I found The Living Well seemed to be completely random but looking back I can now see that having surrendered my life to God, I was ready to go on the next spiritual path I share with you in this book. The first time I saw Sarah I spent some time talking to her and asking questions about God that I really needed to, such as, 'Was God punishing me?', 'Had I done something wrong?', 'Does God punish us to learn?' and 'Why doesn't God stop bad things?' These were all very deep questions that had been within me for some time.

After spending time talking together, Sarah sat and prayed with me in the chapel at The Living Well. I completely broke down and sobbed uncontrollably, almost as if the pain from my childhood was swarming me. But for the first time as I cried and Sarah put her arms around me, I felt wrapped in a love that I had never felt before. It's hard to describe because it was more than the love of physical comfort from another human being; it was a love much deeper than that. I didn't perhaps realise it at the time, but now I think it was the pure love of Jesus that I experienced, as if he was wrapping his arms around me with Sarah's arms. I can't explain how I knew that, but something just felt extraordinarily different.

After that day I began seeing Sarah regularly, and the healing from abuse combined with my growing faith began to take place. I also began to pray, attend worship regularly, and read God's Word. The combination of all those things began to transform my life and the trauma of the abuse began to heal.

I remember at the start of my journey into faith somebody asked me what I wanted. My response was 'I want to find the Anna that God created, not the Anna that had been abused'. I wanted to find my true self and gradually I began to. I think my journey of coming into faith was the pivotal moment of the beginning of my healing. It seemed the significant part of what Jesus proclaimed in his ministry of healing: 'Your faith has made you well'.

Sarah

I was born and brought up in Kenya, the youngest of three girls with a happy childhood blessed with love and freedom. Whilst growing up within a Christian family, my favourite Bible story was the one about the young girl who was thought to be dead and Jesus brought her back to life: Jairus' daughter (Matthew 9:18–26). Over the years this story has come to mean different things to me. As a young person growing up, I was fascinated by the way Jesus brought her to life. At significant times in my own faith journey this passage has been read in churches as one of the gospel readings of the day and I have found myself praying into what it meant on that particular occasion. At times it was as if God was speaking to me about how I am called to bring the life-giving healing of Jesus to myself and my own situations as well as that of others. As I worked at The Living Well I realised that the healing story was speaking to me in a different way. It made me think about how any of us can be paralysed, not just physically, but emotionally and spiritually as well. Any kind of abuse paralyses by the very nature of power, secrecy and the action of abuse. I have seen again and again Jesus coming to those who have been abused and bringing his freedom, his life and his miraculous healing, in the same way he does in this story. I have encountered people paralysed by the effects of abuse they have suffered. I have then seen them stand in a new life and new freedom with Christ where the paralysis of fear, pain and hurt are no longer holding them down.

In the New Testament we see a man who again and again brings life, wholeness and freedom to a variety of people who least expect it. The religious leaders of that day were appalled as Jesus flouted convention and brought healing. It is interesting that in the Greek translation the same word is used for salvation and healing – Sozo. And this is true for those who come to a place of healing from trauma and abuse; because in their healing, very often they also find salvation. This is what happened to Anna as she found herself attending to God for the first time in her life. The key elements for her, as they are with anyone trying to live the Christian life, are prayer, attending worship and reading God's Word. Anna found the cathedral a good place to be and to grow in faith. For others, particularly any who have been abused by those in the church, attending worship or being in a church is almost, if not, wholly impossible. Places such as The Living Well or Crowhurst Christian Healing Centre[b] or even a church where the meeting is informal and takes place in a hall or a school can be easier. The triggers of 'place' can seem less and for some it can then feel safer and easier to engage. It is worth remembering this when we are leading services in our churches.

The journey of healing is never an easy one, as Anna clearly describes in this book. It requires persistence and real courage to walk in the new. It also requires belief that Jesus truly can and does want to bring his healing into our hearts, for all of us in our humanness. Jesus is a companion on the journey. He becomes the 'someone' to share the load with, to sit in the pain with and to help explain the unexplainable. Jesus can help us through the unexplainable concepts such as how does God allow evil and how does he deal with it? What makes it OK? Jesus provides a means to hold onto hope. He is the God who climbs into the pain of abuse with us; he bleeds with us, he cries with us, he hurts with us, all in that place of trauma.

In the Bible, the book of Job can help us to consider our own questions about the nature of God. Job struggles with all that is thrown at him, and yet he still believes in a God who is good and whose nature cannot be known. The important thing is to enable all of us to feel safe enough and free enough to ask the question. To feel allowed to even question God. Why did God not intervene? Where was God in all that I experienced? Why didn't God stop what was happening to me? These are some of the questions that Anna and so many others have asked me. I don't have the answers to these questions but allowing the question is what is important. Reading the book of Job and some commentaries on it can help some people in their understanding of God.

Psalm 44 is sometimes described in the Bible as a 'Psalm of national lament and prayer for help'. At the end of the Psalm the psalmist is asking God why he does not intervene:

'Why do you sleep, O Lord? Awake, do not cast us off forever! Why do you hide your face? Why do you forget our affliction and oppression? For we sink down to the dust; our bodies cling to the ground. Rise up, come to our help. Redeem us for the sake of your steadfast love.' (Psalm 44:23–26)

What is interesting and important is that the psalmist is still talking to God, questioning God, and is in a relationship with God that allows and enables such questions. Being allowed and encouraged to ask the question is more important than the answer.

The choice to decide to believe in a God who did not intervene and did not stop the abuse is always up to each individual. Exploring the possibilities and being honest about the relationship with God is what matters more in someone's healing journey. As David F Ford says:

> *'There comes a point when the questions change. Then we can no longer ask about how to avoid a particular suffering or even why it is happening to us. Instead all our resources are focused on how we might come through it, and our own ultimate question becomes: what is it for? The basic trust is that suffering evil and even death, do not have the last word on life.'* [1]

The sense that death does not have the last word on life gives a different perspective, one that sees life as something more than the experience of the 'now'. There is an eternal perspective in our belief in God that alters how we live and deal with the 'now'. We say many hellos and goodbyes and we can get stuck on the 'goodbye', the death, but in Christ we have life and have it abundantly.

> *'The beauty of the Paschal mystery, the mystery of passing over from the death to life, of moving from goodbye to hello, is that it ends with hello.'* [2]
>
> *(Joyce Rupp).*

This is about holding out the hope that the day will dawn and there will be a new tomorrow. This is the very essence of our faith and, without it, healing could only ever be partial. In Christ, it becomes whole.

I believe the wholeness of healing that Anna found, despite previously having spent many years in therapy, came from the paschal mystery. She had come to partial healing through therapy. However, Jesus brought her healing into wholeness when she let him into that place of trauma within her. That was when her healing began to transform and her faith in Jesus raised her into a place of freedom.

Chapter 3
Understanding Trauma

Sarah

In this chapter Anna shares the complicated impact that trauma has on any individual, especially if that trauma is in childhood. She explores her identity as something that can be lost or changed in the process of abuse. The need to survive and therefore adapt behaviour when faced with repeated trauma can mean that people lose the sense of 'who am I?'

The trauma causes a fracturing within the person, not unlike a broken vase that can be seen as whole and functional or as a series of pieces. These pieces can be referred to as 'parts'. Anna describes the parts of herself which hold her memories and trauma, related to events that happened during her childhood.

Anna

Really exploring my identity was not an easy process. It was complicated! I knew that within me, I had different parts of myself, younger parts that held the trauma and memories of the abuse at different ages. I never quite understood it, but in therapy the younger parts of me were very prominent, wanting to be heard, loved and cared for. But those younger parts always felt very stuck. They were stuck in the trauma, almost perpetually reliving it. I never had a sense of how that could change; I just thought that that was the way I'd always be. There was the adult part of me that was fully functioning, able to hold down a responsible job and manage day-to-day life, and then the little parts of me still sobbing inside from being abused, terrified and paralysed in fear. I didn't think it could ever change; I just thought I'd always live with it all like that inside me. It never had changed in all my years of therapy.

I thought about the identities of people in the Bible. And I thought about God as the Trinity, as three-in-one, which is one of the greatest mysteries of God! But it seems that in his image, we all have capacity to hold different identities at the same time. For example, I am a daughter, a sister and a niece. And we all use different parts of our identities at different times, as we need to. In the Bible, God gives some people new names as their identities change. For example, Sarai in the book of Genesis becomes Sarah when she becomes a mother (Genesis 17:15), and Abram becomes Abraham the father of all generations (Genesis 17:5). Jesus gives some of his disciples new names when he calls them to follow him. And Saul becomes Paul after he is transformed by God on the road to Damascus (Acts 13:9).

I realised that part of my identity became fragmented as a child because of the abuse I suffered. As a child, it was impossible to bear all the pain as a whole. I understood that the little parts within me were the parts which had sort of been split off from me at the time of abuse so that I could survive. So those parts held the physical and emotional memories. That had helped my adult part to grow, survive and separate, on one level, from the abuse. And the reason why those little parts of me were so stuck is because those parts were still in the trauma of abuse.

But early on whilst going to see Sarah something fundamentally began to change that. I can't explain how, but I can describe what happened.

On one occasion when I went to see Sarah, one of the little parts of me was very prominent in talking to her. That part of me was crying and distressed. But during this encounter Sarah asked the little part of me 'What is your name?'

I can't put into words how significant that question was. She asked the little part of me directly 'What is your name?

The response that came back was, 'Anna, just Anna'. The encounter wasn't anything to do with the name; it was fundamentally something to do with reaching out to the little wounded parts of me and speaking directly to them, connecting with them. No one else had ever done that.

It reminds me of the story of Jesus meeting the man possessed by demons (Luke 8:26–35). Because of his 'demons', this man had been excluded from society, chained down and not even allowed to wear clothes. But when Jesus encountered him, he asked the man 'What is your name?'

In that moment, as the wounded man encounters Jesus he is able to speak directly back to Jesus and to share his identity with him: 'Legion', he replies. Jesus gets to know him – his true identity. Jesus frees him and heals him. The little parts within me were not 'demons' or 'unclean spirits' that needed to be removed from me. But the little parts of me were my fragmented child self that needed to be set free in a completely different way. It is important from my perspective that Christians do not confuse this. It must be understood properly and understood as trauma.

So, when Sarah asked the little part of me, 'What is your name?' it was also transforming for me. The encounter opened up the truth of my whole identity. The little parts of me were still locked in the trauma. The moments where I dissociated from the pain of abuse were still frozen in the little parts of me. But as Sarah, with Jesus, reached into those parts within me, it was as if the light of Christ came into the centre of my core, allowing all of my identity to be seen and heard. And in that transformative moment, it was the beginning of us, all of me, being able to sit with Jesus clothed in his love.

And that's exactly what happened as time went on. Sarah began to get to know each part of me that was still in immense pain from being abused. She listened, she comforted, she prayed. We cried, we screamed, we sobbed. Over time each part began to laugh and play. We began bit by bit to share those moments that had been frozen and in the light and love of Jesus each part slowly began to integrate within me and the pain started to evaporate. What I never believed could change, over time miraculously began to. It was so important to understand my whole identity in my healing in order to begin to find and understand more about the Anna that God created. My identity had been fragmented in the trauma, but those parts were all part of me. Unlocking those parts to free them from the trauma enabled me to begin to see what those parts brought to me as a whole – the whole Anna, who God created.

Sarah

> *'That morning I realised I would probably spend the rest of my professional life trying to unravel the mysteries of trauma. How do horrific experiences cause people to become hopelessly stuck in the past? What happens to people's minds and brains that keeps them frozen, trapped in a place they desperately wish to escape.'* [3]
>
> *(Van der Kolk)*

I echo the words of Bessel Van Der Kolk. Understanding disassociation and trauma is mysterious and complex. But there is also so much hope for repair and healing. I find there is still so much that can't be explained because every person I have ever worked with is different from another.

When I think about the Christian faith, Christians have been trying to explain the nature of the Trinity for the past 2,000 years, yet we are still exploring what it means and how to describe it in modern day times. And so it is with trauma and healing.

I am constantly amazed at how clever creation is, for the way we survive trauma. Our minds and bodies have capacity to block out terrifying experiences to survive the movement of abuse. Neuroscience helps us to understand that trauma – physical, emotional and sexual – is all remembered within the person, but a part of the person holds the trauma within themselves, in a fragmented way. This is known in medical terms as Dissociative Identity Disorder (DID). Most of the people that I've worked with have survived abuse in this way. The acceptance and knowledge of having parts varies with each individual that I've supported. I have worked with some people who are 'co-conscious' all the time. This means that if a part of the person is talking or sharing something, then their adult 'main' part is fully aware of all that is said and is going on. I have also worked with others who have no recollection that they have a part or any interaction that has happened; they just know that they lose time and, for example, find themselves in places where they had not set out to go when leaving home. This makes life very complicated and frightening as so much of their day becomes blank which can then feel re-traumatising. Identity becomes confused as the person is not sure who they really are. It is not just the 'who am I at work today?' question. But a fundamental 'who am I today?'

It is usually the adult person who comes first to see me, and some therapists call this the 'host' part. The adult part is often trying to make sense of their world, which feels confusing to them. People describe themselves as feeling anxious or angry and have no idea why. This makes the person wonder what is happening inside them and their internal world. For some people one of their parts will be the driving force in making changes, engaging with therapy, or the healing process. It is usually when something happens or the person has a health scare that there is a sense of confusion, as it reactivates the trauma. It is at this point the person sometimes seeks mental health care or decides to go on their own journey of exploration, which is when people tend to seek my support.

As the exploration begins, there is a gradual realisation that there are other parts, voices, ways of being and doing things within the one person. This is very different from any kind of psychosis and must not be confused with it. With psychosis the belief and behaviour is irrational and cannot be explained, and fundamentally is not the result of childhood trauma. There is a rationality in the person with DID that I have never seen in someone who is psychotic. It is possible to bring the person back to the here and now, into the present with an increased understanding of who they are. Psychosis is irrational and usually includes visual or auditory hallucinations and there is no sense to be made in what is said or seen – there is an unconnectivity in it all.

In DID, the different parts of a person remain locked in trauma until something releases. So much about abuse is about secrecy, keeping quiet and never telling. Therefore, the part has to feel safe before anything can be explored – safe in their adult self as well as safe in the world they live in. In my experience there needs to be a deep knowing that whatever happened, however awful it was, it is not happening now and has not happened for some time. It is an inner understanding of the fact that the abuse is 'over'. I have been there as parts are free enough to speak to me, to share something of the awfulness of what they hold, to encourage them to be themselves and to have their own identity.

With Anna it was the 6-year-old part of her who felt free enough and safe enough to talk first before the other parts began to connect with me. I often think of a small child who is abused, threatened, beaten or tortured. As humans we use the same animal response of 'freeze'/'playing dead' in order to survive. The pain of the event is frozen. The adult carries that frozen memory for life or until they begin to ask questions such as 'Why do I always have a panic attack in rooms where the door is locked, and the curtains are shut?' Or 'Why do my feet feel very sensitive and I hate others touching them?' As these questions are explored and as they look at their responses in situations that should be safe, which still feel threatening, the person gradually realises that there is a cause for how they respond and feel. This allows the different parts to begin to share something of the trauma. When I asked 6-year-old Anna her name I did so because with other people I have worked with they have had a series of names for their parts often without the adult part even knowing. Sometimes the part has the name which describes how they feel, such as 'shame', 'bad girl', 'stupid' or 'brainy'. As the parts share and own the trauma, I have witnessed people feeling released from the impact of it. This takes time and energy as is described later in the book; it requires a sense of acceptance and understanding of the truth.

The parts formed in trauma need to be released from the trauma they are holding. It is an acceptance of the trauma that enables the adult part to begin to allow the other parts of themselves to express what is going on. In the early days of being alongside Anna it was the very small part that was able to say how frightened she was and in holding her through that and repeatedly saying 'the bad people' who did this to her have gone away forever, she was able to relax and over time felt able to do normal things without feeling terrified. The key as far as I am concerned is to love that part and go on loving that part until that part knows how safe they are. For me this is the essence of Jesus' ministry and how I try to follow him. In 1 John 4:16–17 (Youth Bible) it says, 'God is love. Those who live in love live in God, and God lives in them. This is how love is made perfect in us.'

There must be a building up of trust so that new memories can be made. But it is also important that the adult part can start to look after the younger parts within themselves. At times I have asked adult parts, 'Why are you so dismissive of this part or why are you so negative towards him? He has held this trauma for you all this time.' It is often the adult part that struggles because if they have to acknowledge the other parts within them, the adult part has to believe and be faced with the reality of the abuse. That can be daunting and frightening. However, if this can be done, the parts will grow settled, knowing they're safe. If the adult part continues to ignore the other parts, healing is only partial because the trauma remains stuck. To heal, the parts have to be acknowledged and heard and released and loved through the process. Sadly, I have found no shortcuts in the 'doing' of this process.

To understand what it is like to sit alongside someone as they share their experiences is more than just to understand it in neuro-scientific or psychological terms. It is about understanding it from the perspective of the part: 2-year-old Anna or 6-year-old Anna. It is about hearing the awfulness of their abuse and bringing reassurance, healing and love.

And that is the mystery – to bring the love of Christ into the small and adult part of each person who has suffered abuse. Because as the light of Christ is brought into each part, I have seen something of the amazing love of God that comes to heal and transform. It is beyond explanation. It is mystery of the most extraordinary sort. We can't explain the workings of God. In my ministry with people who have suffered abuse, I have sat alongside the healing of traumatised parts of people in awe, wonder and love.

Chapter 4
Learning about Truth

Sarah

In this chapter Anna explores the difficulties of facing the truth about those who abused her and living daily with that truth. Pilate asked Jesus, 'What is truth?' (John 18:38). Here Anna explores that question for herself.

Anna

With the beginnings of my new-found faith, and as I began to unlock the trauma within me, I questioned what that meant for me in my healing journey and having a relationship with God. In the early stages of developing a relationship with God, each time I had a knock-back or a setback, or the pain of healing overwhelmed me, I instinctively wanted to walk away from God, and believe that I was once again alone in the world and could survive alone. My pattern of surviving abuse had been to 'freeze'. It had enabled my mind and body to shut down when being abused. So, when I was faced with difficulties after coming into my faith, I found that I also wanted to 'freeze' in my relationship with God. I wanted to pretend He didn't exist, as I had wanted to pretend the abuse had never happened.

Everyone's journey into faith is different; my spiritual journey at this early stage felt fast-paced and I felt like I was tested over and over again in quick succession. Things would happen that would try and pull me back or hurt me or distract me. I began to realise that I was being pulled back into old patterns and thoughts and it was very intense. It would sometimes lead me to a place of complete despair; a place of doubting, crying uncontrollably, feeling useless and wondering if things could ever truly be better for me.

At times when I had these feelings, I felt suicidal. It was a feeling I'd had as a teenager when I'd not known a way out. The same feeling resurfaced every now and then as an adult. I think I had learnt over the years to manage suicidal feelings. I knew that when I reached that dark place, I had to seek help and talk my way back through it. I often phoned the Samaritans[c] at those times. I found that talking my way through it was a way for me to gather myself so I could then walk through to the other side. Maybe ignorantly, I was surprised that with the huge leaps in faith I'd made, the suicidal feelings still surfaced. I assumed that with my new understanding of how God viewed human life and His plans for each of us, it would have perhaps eradicated my feelings of suicide. But it didn't and I quickly realised that we're all fallible in a human world. However, by having God in my life, it enabled me to gather myself through the points of despair in a different way, an easier way perhaps.

So, how did it make it easier? And how did my faith challenge my old patterns of managing trauma and pain? What I began to realise was that now I had the presence of the Holy Spirit, 'freezing' had actually become impossible. It's hard to describe in words what I mean by that. But as I surrendered to God and asked Him to lead me, I began to feel His presence with me. Therefore, pretending God did not exist did not really feel possible. It was ultimately a choice I made – to trust in God. God would never leave me, but I have the free will to turn away from Him. It was my choice to stay with Him and, in that choice, I found I could no longer use my 'freeze' response.

I became faced with a dilemma – if I don't 'freeze' in the face of pain and adversity, what do I do now? How do I trust God to help me through it and how do I believe He can when no one had helped me as a child? In my new experience of not being able to 'freeze' anymore, these were tricky dilemmas I found myself in. I seemed to enter what I now know as 'spiritual battles' whereby I felt very tested in who and what I was going to trust in. At this early point in my faith and healing I found myself reading the passage in the Bible of the temptation of Jesus over and over again (Matthew 4:1–11). I didn't understand why I was reading this at the time, but

I can see why now. It gave me wisdom in that early testing stage of my faith. Jesus was faced with his own internal battles in the wilderness, just as I was at this stage, but in a very different way.

I think my experience at that time could be seen as very wilderness-like. It's interesting to think about some of the stories of people finding themselves in the wilderness in the Bible. The story that seems most striking to me is when God freed his people from slavery and oppression in Egypt. He enabled Moses to lead the people through the parting of the Red Sea and then into the freedom of the wilderness (Exodus 14). On the face of it, the story reads of how very quickly the people complained after being freed because they didn't know how they could survive. To the reader, the people almost seem ungrateful that they had been freed because they had found themselves in an unknown territory of the wilderness. They even wished at one stage they could return to the slavery they had once known (Exodus 16). It is not uncommon for victims of abuse to return to abusive situations or people that have abused them. This isn't because they are weak or silly. It's because sometimes for survivors of abuse it's all they've known and the thought of freedom, however safe that might be, is also very scary because it is so unfamiliar. The story of Exodus describes that human reaction so well.

Underneath that seeming ungratefulness, the emotions of the freed people resonated with me – the fear of the unknown, needing to learn to trust in a whole new way of living and to find a reliance on God. When we read the story of Exodus, the glory of God to free his oppressed people is clear to see. But for the people, they went through all the range of human emotions such as doubt, uncertainty and fear. They too, as I was, had to learn how to navigate a new life and put dependence and reliance in God.

Rowan Williams in his book talks about how fundamental learning to trust God is when we consider our belief in God:

'Basic to everything here is the idea that Christian belief is really about knowing who and what to trust.' [4]

I would say that one of the most important things I did at the beginning of this journey, which helped me to navigate my way through these dilemmas, was to learn about 'truth'.

Truth had meant different things along the way; speaking the truth of the abuse, learning the truth about God, understanding the truth of who I am in God, accepting the truth about others as well as myself, being true to myself... and much more.

One of the first things I needed to realise was that even when I'd been abused, God had been there, feeling the hurt each time I was hurt. I have this image in my head of God and the angels gasping at the moment an act of abuse is carried out, gasping in pain and agony when a human being chooses to hurt another. Initially, that was a hard concept to understand. But that's where knowing God and therefore knowing the truth about God was important. God did not create us as human beings that He controlled; He created us to have free will. That is evident from the story of the Fall in the Garden of Eden, where Adam and Eve acted of their own free will (Genesis 3). Therefore, understanding that when someone abused me it was an act of free will, a choice they made – a very wrong choice. It meant that I now understood that God did not control the decisions people made to abuse me. Understanding the act of abuse in this way for the first time in my life meant that I laid the blame with the abuser rather than with me or with God for allowing it to happen. The blame sat with the person it rightly should sit with and that is the abuser – the person who, from their own free will, chose to abuse.

Understanding God had created human beings with free will enabled me to understand the truth of God's position in the abuse – that he had had no part in it. This then freed my relationship with God to look at how he could help me to heal from the abuse. By knowing that God had no part in the abuse, I was now able to see that he could have a part in helping me out of the trauma, and that was in fact where I found some 'hope'.

Hope – it was a very new concept after my brain had been programmed to feel 'hopeless' for so long, but what a wonderful new concept I had found.

Having hope was one way that helped to gather me in times of despair as well as knowing that with God I had choices to make. Previously, without turning to God in times of despair, I had to find something of myself to help me, which isn't easy when you are in a place of despair and feeling so awful. It was a real test of my new faith to understand these choices I had when feeling in a dark place. I began to understand that God is a God of love, hope and freedom. He isn't a God of worry or doubt or confusion. So, when those latter feelings began creeping inside me during times of despair, I began to see that sinking into those feelings was taking me further away from God, and therefore further away from hope and love and freedom. When I felt that happening I began to actively make a choice to walk with God, however painful it may be, because I knew sinking in the other direction would be pretty bleak. In making the decision to walk with God (which sometimes meant saying aloud, 'hold my hand Jesus'), I was then able to ask for his help and comfort in my darkest moments instead of trying to battle through alone. That was where my pattern of freezing began to break. I didn't need to retreat and hide and do this alone: I could now ask for help. It wasn't easy and from my experience the release of pain is not always immediate. But choosing in that moment to stay with God rather than be stuck helped me to remain calm in a place of despair for the first time in my life. I knew I could walk free holding Jesus' hand.

I was learning to rely on God for strength and somehow this began to break my patterns of coping with the trauma. I realised it was no longer sustainable for me to rely on my own strength. In my healing, I was now learning that the one being I needed to break these old patterns of surviving was God.

Sarah's role in my understanding of all this was crucial. Sarah initially had to hold the truth and hope for me. She often repeated

God's truth to me when I was in a dark place and through many tears and times of pain, she would guide me to God in prayer. But also, through the comfort she provided to me. Sarah always waited with me through the times of distress and pain, often holding me and hugging me. This is something that I had never experienced as a child. When I had been abused, I had no one to comfort me after the pain, which is how I had learnt to shut down emotionally and physically. But this time when talking through some of the memories or feeling the pain of the memories physically, Sarah provided all the comfort I had never had at the time. Sarah stayed with me in the pain until it began to ease. Over time, I felt it shifted the way I coped with the pain, knowing that I could go through it and eventually be calm and walk on with Jesus. This healing, alongside my growing knowledge of God, enabled me to face my pain and come through it in a completely new way.

Sarah

Standing in the truth, and staying with the truth, is essential for our healing. When survivors of abuse start living in the truth instead of the lies, I have seen how the work of the Holy Spirit begins to bring them into greater freedom. However, at this stage of the healing journey, there is something interesting that happens, when old patterns of coping and surviving also get challenged. Many people who have been abused have coped by freezing to block out the pain of what is happening to them. However, the fruits of the Holy Spirit 'love, joy, peace, patience, kindness, generosity, faithfulness, gentleness and self-control' (Galatians 5:22–23), do not fit with the moment of 'freeze' response to trauma. I have witnessed in my work with survivors of abuse that as the person is held in love emotionally as well as, at times, physically, it seems to break the 'freeze'. I have witnessed how it is impossible for people to stay 'frozen' in such circumstances. As Anna shared her 'freeze' moments so she stayed in them until she was then safe.

It reminds me of the story of the storm (Matthew 14:22–33). In the story, the disciples are in the boat and there is a storm raging.

They must have wondered what on earth was going on. There are times in life when there are storms. There are times that I know and sense that Anna or someone else is experiencing a real storm where it feels as if all they are going through or accessing or remembering is overwhelming. At such times all I can do is remind the person that, however it feels, Jesus is with them and will come across the water to their place of feeling overwhelmed.

The disciples were terrified in this story and so much of abuse is about fear. When we are very frightened all our senses work differently and we can jump to conclusions; no wonder the disciples thought Jesus was a ghost. Then in the reality of knowing that Jesus is with us, whatever the storm we are experiencing, we, like Peter, are called to go on trusting, to trust and to trust and to trust again. So, we step out of the boat. Engaging in our own healing is very like stepping out of the boat. We are trusting Jesus to be there, to hold us, even in the worst of our storms of life. Jesus holds us again and again as we work through the memories and the pain that has been stored for so long and which God longs to bring His healing into. He comes to hold us in those moments of feeling overwhelmed, when we've taken the courage to step out and trust in Him.

This 'being' with the person is part of the healing journey and I always pray at the end of my time with the people I am with. Often it's a very short prayer because we are all tired, but I claim the love and presence and healing of Jesus in all that has been shared and has happened. Time and again people say to me it's the prayer at the end that seals what has happened, that makes it all real and, in some cases, makes it all OK.

Anna

So, I had begun to change the way I understood things, both about the abuse and about God. The next thing I had to learn was the truth about who I was and not the lies that had been put into me each time I was abused.

God had not made me to be abused – that was a fundamental thing to understand. God doesn't bring anyone into this world to be abused. Human life abuses us, not God. When I realised this, I realised I wanted to find the Anna that God created and not the Anna that had been abused. Because I had suffered abuse since I was a baby, I had little concept of the Anna that had not been abused and that was incredibly sad. For years and years, I had certain phrases that I said about myself including 'I'm horrible, I'm stupid, I'm useless, I'm unloveable... ' With help from Sarah and my growing knowledge of God I began to recognise that these phrases weren't truth, they were in fact lies. I realised they were words that represented how my parents had left me feeling and how I had made sense of the abuse from such a young age: 'It must have been because I was horrible; it must have been because I was stupid.' That's how my mind had become programmed for over 30 years. However, when I began to look at God's truth, what He says about every human being, I realised that all the things I was calling myself had created a false identity, a myth.

God's truth is – I am a loved child of God. God did not want me to be abused; he didn't build the human race to abuse and hurt children. People had said to me for years that the abuse wasn't my fault. So why had I never truly believed it, and why are people who have been abused not going to believe it for themselves? Twenty years in and out of therapy hadn't helped me come to that place of truly believing the abuse wasn't my fault. So what was different now?

We all hope to grow up with a sense of security and love. But like so many others, I hadn't had that. Instead I had grown up in fear, confusion and worry. My parents said they loved me even though they abused me. So, I grew up thinking that love and hurt just came together as one. I hadn't experienced anything different from that. Deep down I always knew the way I was being hurt was wrong, but somehow I'd blamed myself. That was until I understood that the concept of love, according to God, means we *don't* hurt another.

So, I began to see that love and hurt didn't come together in one package, as I'd grown up believing.

No one had ever given me the fundamental answer to whether people can love and hurt you at the same time. I hadn't found that answer in therapy or through any other support I'd accessed. I'd only seen Sarah a couple of times, I think, when I asked her the question 'If you love someone can you hurt them?' This time I got the answer! 'No,' she replied. Her answer was simple: 'No'. It didn't appear to need expanding on. So I then asked the next, more difficult, question. 'Does that mean my mum and dad didn't love me?' I wasn't entirely sure if I wanted the answer and I don't recall Sarah's exact words. But in a roundabout way she answered 'yes'. That answer hurt; it was a harsh reality. But I knew that Sarah's answer wasn't anything to do with her own judgements about my parents; her answer had come from the truth about love according to God.

Maybe my parents had wished to love me, but their choice to abuse me had not been loving in any way. Choosing to abuse me meant that they had not loved me. True love means that there is no way you would want to hurt someone – I mean intentional hurt, abuse. I remember having a conversation with my therapist not long after I'd had this discussion with Sarah. In explaining my new understanding, my therapist asked me something along the lines of 'What if they didn't mean to hurt you?' (She was in no way condoning the abuse, by the way, but was trying to tease out my new understanding.) But I answered her so clearly and precisely, saying, 'Then they would have apologised and chosen not to do it again and again'. And that was the truth about love. You wouldn't want to do anything that caused anyone pain, let alone cause pain over and over again. Love is about care and warmth and protection and growing. Abuse is about pain and hurt and confusion and terror. The two are completely different.

Therefore I understood the abuse I'd suffered for the first time in its true nature as abuse and not caught between this whole enmeshed 'love and hurt' state that had been muddled in my head every time I'd been abused. And in understanding that, I slowly began to see that it wasn't anything I had done; it was a choice my parents had made, a very wrong choice. It allowed me to see that by God creating human beings to have free will, some people could make the wrong choices. My parents had done that and therefore the fault of the abuse lay with them and them alone.

As I look back now at the journey, I can see how fundamental it was to learn the truth about God and who I am in Him at the beginning of this process. I'm not sure the next step could have been taken for me, without having established this first. Within a few months of seeing Sarah I had let God into my life, developed a growing sense of the truth of God and had begun to let the truth about me in relationship to God emerge. I had then started to think it would be possible to let go of the lies that had created a false identity in me each time I'd been abused.

As I came to see Sarah in these early days it felt very much like being led to Jesus. In John 14:6 Jesus said 'I am the way, and the truth, and the life.' Jesus was, in an unexplainable way, showing me the way, the truth and my life in him. This was worlds apart from how I'd grown up and developed my life into adulthood. But now I was able to see that my identity had been falsely created by the lies of the abuse and the people who had abused me. I was beginning to see that my new life in Christ was about being truly loved and that this love was completely based on truth.

Sarah

Abuse is, by its very nature full of lies. Speaking the truth is absolutely essential in the process of healing from abuse whatever the faith of the person or even if they have no faith. When someone has been abused, there have been so many lies told, often for so long. For example, 'this is safe', 'this is our secret', 'this is normal', 'this is OK'. The abuse of another person is never OK; it is never 'normal'; it is never whatever is said to make it seem right. Part of the abuse is what is said to the person, what I call 'one-liners'. For example, 'you are bad', 'you are useless', 'this is all your fault'.

Within the process of healing, my work has been to enable survivors to challenge these lies and find out if there is truth in any of the statements that have been said by the abuser. This work is carried out from the Christian perspective, that the person is a 'loved child of God'. But even for those with no faith, understanding the lies and not living in them is so important.

In working with brokenness, the truth needs to be explored. People say things such as 'He seemed such a nice man'; 'No one would ever have thought he could do this'; 'He was a priest'; 'He was a doctor'; 'He was my dad so how could I believe this about him?'; 'Perhaps all my memories are wrong'. These and many other statements have been spoken to me many times and I have found that it is important to reply in ways such as 'Yes he was your dad, but he chose to do this too. Yes, he was a doctor and he abused the position of power that he had. He chose to do wrong and evil things to you and pretend they were alright.' The recent abuse cases in the media such as Jimmy Saville and others, and those in the church, show only too clearly how easy it is for us all to believe the lie and to think 'surely that could never have happened.' When in fact it *did* happen and it was very wrong.

In abuse situations the truth has been blurred, often with such words such as 'this is for your own good'. That is a lie; no abuse or harm to another can ever be for their own good. In abuse situations the action sometimes accompanies the words, 'I love you, I am only doing this to show you I love you. This is about you being my special girl. I am teaching you about love.' I want to write in capitals LIES! LIES! LIES! Abuse, sexual harm, physical harm, emotional harm, is never about love and is never for the person's good. When someone has heard a lot of such lies over and over and over for many years, it blurs the truth and the truth becomes very difficult, if not impossible, to see.

It's important to help the person to feel safe even if the memories are horrible and feel difficult to deal with. The person I'm with has to consider what truth feels like, what safe feels like and the truth that no one is hurting them now. They also have to learn whether what I or anyone else is saying to them has an authenticity about it.

Learning to trust how it feels to be safe and in the truth is difficult because after abuse it has to be relearnt. A survivor of abuse was often told by the abuser that they were safe, and they were not. So, working out what is different about feeling safe in the present is so important. Reassuring people that they are free to walk out at any time and no one is making them stay in the room can be helpful as it gives the survivor choice. It helps the person to distinguish between the past and understand that the present moment is not abusive.

Survivors of abuse very often feel that they want their dad or doctor or priest to be the person that they expected them to be and to have their best welfare at their heart. Sadly, sitting in the truth means that the survivor has to come to a place of acceptance that the person chose to behave in a way that was wrong and was not in their best interests at all. Sometimes that truth is hard to accept, and this can mean people choose to stay in a place of denial. It could be argued that Judas did not want to accept the truth that Jesus would be condemned and crucified. So too, the Pharisees seemed unable to accept that Jesus could possibly be the Messiah. Sometimes victims of abuse find it safer to remain in denial and that is a choice they are free to make.

Jesus talked about the truth setting us free, 'you will know the truth, and the truth will make you free.' (John 8:32). 'I came that they may have life, and have it abundantly.' (John 10:10). 'I am the way, and the truth, and the life.' (John 14:6). What does Jesus mean when he says this? It means that following Jesus brings us to a place of truth. Yes, we have to face ourselves as well as the truth about our past, even the parts of our personalities we don't like. It is about recognising how truth changes who we are as well as how we behave. An example of this is found in the musical *Les Miserables*[5] where it is expressed in song very appropriately: there is a part where Fantine sings 'I dreamed that love would never die. I dreamed that God would be forgiving'. In the finale Valjean, Fantine and Eponine all sing 'Take my hand and lead me to salvation. Take my love for love is everlasting. And remember the truth that once was spoken to love another person is to see the face of God.' This quote explains much better than I can about love and truth.

What Anna was doing at this stage in her healing was to explore anew the truth about the relationships around her, including the painful truth of the relationships with those that abused her.

Living in denial is as much of a lie as denying the abuse that happened. Sometimes people are unable to accept the healing either through the therapeutic relationship or from God because they are in denial. Denial that the abuse ever happened, denial that it matters, denial that they have the right to see it differently, denial that they can live a life that is fulfilled and fulfilling.

With some people, facing the truth – the truth that the adults in their world chose to abuse them and to lie to them – is too much to bear. For some people, being in denial is easier to cope with than facing the truth. That is always the individual's choice. I have heard people talk about abuse as if it didn't matter because it was not as bad as some of the other things that happened. But the truth is that it was very bad, it should never have happened, and it is not helpful to judge the level of abuse in this way. For me abuse is abuse and is wrong and very harmful. Minimising it to cope is not a lasting healing.

Chapter 5
Integration – Living in Harmony

Sarah

In this chapter Anna describes how she began to love all the parts of herself that had been formed in the trauma of her abuse. The way in which Anna did this is not the only way to live with dissociated parts; others have found different ways. It is unique to each person. The important part of the process is to acknowledge the parts of self and love them.

In my work with people over the years, one of the main features is having faith in a loving, healing God for both me and the person I am working with. As each part of the person in their own unique way learns about the love of Christ and feels something of the light that can dispel the darkness, the power of love over fear, so the parts have a new identity in common. Instead of the only identity being one of shared memories of abuse it is one of a new relationship with Jesus. This can be explored and shared in the process. The difference of how to share is more to do with the age and understanding. A 6-year-old asks different questions about faith compared to a teenager or an adult. The growing understanding of all that Jesus is and does builds a new relationship that, in itself, is both loving and healing and that helps the parts to relate to each other in a new way.

Anna

The healing of the little parts of me began to shift in a way they never had before. It felt like it happened at quite a pace once the parts of me began talking to and sharing things with Sarah. Sarah understood me, – the adult and all the little parts, and I was beginning to feel more whole as a result. Instead of the different parts of me feeling disjointed as we always had, it was as if I was beginning to link all the traumatised parts of me to my adult self. 'Wholeness of healing' is a common phrase I had heard, and I really began to understand what that meant for me. It was like an internal wholeness developing from within, inside my core, my soul perhaps? It was a process that was completely different to therapy.

There were a series of events that took place in quite quick succession when the process of integration within me began to happen.

I had been taking daily walks to the beach as things in my life began to change. On these walks I found that I would start chatting to God and Jesus in my head. I would say how I was feeling, talk about the day, and ask God to help me with things I just couldn't understand or didn't know what to do about. I didn't know it at the time, but this was how I first started to pray.

On one particular day, I knew the 2-year-old part of me was feeling very fragile and was struggling with memories. So, I began talking to God about the pain the 2-year-old was in and the feelings that part of me had. I had always felt the pain; it was a neediness, a longing, an intense pain in the core of my body. It was a feeling I had always had, and it had always felt very dominant. As I spoke about it with God, I began to realise how perpetuating the feeling was, like something going round and round inside me but never being able to escape. As I spoke to God in my head, it was like a light bulb had been switched on and I could see the way ahead, see what I'd never seen before. I realised that the only way to relieve the pain for the 2-year-old was to start letting go of the abuse and the memories she had. I realised that by not letting go, the little 2-year-old within me continued to re-experience the abuse. That realisation was painful, but it hit me, jolted me out of the way I'd always been surviving. Up until that moment, the little parts of me had just walked on in life with me, but they had been carrying the weight of this, carrying the burden of abuse put on to me each time I was abused. That burden had become immense and the little parts were cloaked in it all. They were still there, almost living it from that exact time the abuse happened – still frozen in the trauma. I could suddenly see why I had always felt stuck.

God's wisdom jolted me in a way I'd never been jolted before; it was as if an internal instinct kicked in, deep within me. I remember so clearly deciding at that moment of being jolted that there was no way I could continue to allow the little parts of me to re-experience the abuse or carry the heavy burden of it. I made a declaration to God that I now needed to start letting the little parts of me be free to be the little ones they had never been before. It felt like Jesus and I had scooped up the little 2-year-old part of me and for the first time said to her 'you don't have to be abused anymore'. So, with Sarah, I did begin finding a way to let go, for all the parts of me. That was a significant process that I describe in chapter 7.

Not long after this significant moment of realisation happened, a second very powerful moment happened. I think the more that the little parts of me started to really feel loved and cared for by Jesus and Sarah, the more I as the adult was allowing myself to really get to know these other parts of myself. Up until then, I'd tried to keep these parts at a distance in my mind because they held the trauma of the abuse we suffered. However, the more Jesus and Sarah were beginning to love these parts of me, the more I was beginning to see I could love these parts of me too. One night while sitting in bed I was thinking about the little parts of me and, all of a sudden, I decided I needed to bring all those parts of me into bed with me. It may sound an odd thing, but it was this very visual representation in my head of taking all the little parts of me out of the beds and cots where they had been stuck and terrified and bringing them into the safety of my home in the 'here and now', into my bed where it was safe and where we could all sleep in peace.

That evening was an incredibly powerful moment of healing because it felt like I was integrating every part back inside me. And in doing so, something intrinsically different happened within me which was beyond explanation. The most amazing thing was that the next morning when I woke up, it felt quiet inside me. It was the first thing I noticed when I woke... that it was quiet. It was only then that I realised every day, for as long as I could remember, I had woken up with the little parts of me screaming and crying within me. To wake up in peace, where every part of me was in peace felt miraculous, the most wonderful feeling.

After the significant moment of emotionally claiming all the little parts inside me, I began to live with all the little parts of me and myself as the adult. How did that feel? It felt surreal, beautiful and unknown! I realised just how much I loved all these parts of me and how very protective I felt about them. However, I had never lived my life so integrated as I'd survived by splitting off these parts. So, it was like learning to live all over again. I suddenly felt vulnerable in situations that wouldn't have usually bothered me; I felt exhausted doing things that I wouldn't normally have to think about, and I had to listen to myself in ways I'd never had to before. It was time-consuming. Every part of me was adjusting, needed different things and I had to spend time *really* getting to know each part of me. I felt this odd pressure to get things right because I felt so protective in having brought these parts into myself. I think the pressure was about the adult part of me that had learnt to get things right as I'd never been free to get things wrong and be OK. But there was also something inside me that just wanted to love and care for these parts of me that had never experienced love and care before. I think the love of Jesus and Sarah was really at the heart of this and with every step I took, they were there guiding me. During the months before this moment happened, I had experienced both the genuine love and care that Sarah was showing all of me as well as her praying directly with each part of me. Through the way in which Sarah cared about each part of me, I began to learn how to care for them too. This was beyond therapy; it was a deeply spiritual process which had God's true love at its centre.

As time went on, I gradually noticed that the little parts of me were not only integrating with me as an adult but also with each other. It was like a unity was forming within me. It's hard to describe but some of these moments were felt most poignantly when I attended different services at the cathedral. One evening I went to a healing service on the feast day of St Luke, which was being led by Sarah. At around that time, the very little part of me, a baby, had been experiencing some very difficult body memories and was in quite a lot of pain physically and emotionally. The 10-year-old part of me had really wanted to go to the service as she wanted to go and support Sarah. So, we went. It was a beautiful service in the crypt, lit with candles and lots of really peaceful music. During the service people were invited to go for prayer. We stayed sitting where we were and listened to the music whilst others went for prayer. As we sat and listened to the music, I prayed for God to help the baby part of me with the pain she was experiencing. The pain had felt excruciating at times. It was as if, by feeling safer, the bodily memories were free to come out for the first time. I have found bodily memories to be some of the most painful memories to experience because there is often not a cognitive memory as with the older child parts of me, but it is just a reliving of the physical pain. But as I sat praying to God about the pains there was a beautiful moment whereby all the other little parts of me said how much they loved the little baby within us and wanted to help her. We all sat together, internally cuddling Baby Girl, almost the image of a family cooing over a newborn baby. We all said silently to Baby Girl that we wanted to help her to be happy and loved in a way she never was. And with that, we felt Baby Girl smile in our arms. It was such a profound and gentle moment. I really felt like Jesus was helping us learn to love each other and brought his own love, right there in that moment to Baby Girl. It is a moment of healing that will never leave me. It was a binding together of old wounds that had been so separate within me, now bound together in the love of Jesus.

I think that moment was also the first moment in noticing that all the parts of me could start functioning together rather than existing as the disjointed parts we had been. And in being able to function together I felt we could start healing in a different way. There was individual healing to be done, but there was also some integrative healing starting.

I had never wanted to get caught up in labels or diagnoses because I had a strong sense that I needed to lead my own journey with all the little parts of me and to follow the journey God was taking me on. That required a capacity to really listen to God and to myself. There were many more powerful moments where all the parts of me became further and further integrated. In my experience, bringing Jesus into the centre of that was fundamental.

I can recall another particular service at the cathedral very vividly. Every part of me enjoyed worshipping there and it was a place where we could feel safe and comfortable. There was often a particular way it felt like we all sat: 2-year-old and 6-year-old sat on my lap, Anna Girl and later on Teenage Anna, sat either side of me, Anna Girl linking her arm in mine and next to them Jesus sat holding Baby Girl in his arms. Obviously, no one else had a clue of this visual image of all of me, but weirdly during this stage of our healing, more often than not the seat next to me always remained empty, seemingly left for Jesus! But I also think it allowed us the space we needed at the time.

Anyhow, on this particular day, it was the feast day of the baptism of Jesus. It evoked all sorts of feelings for Baby Girl knowing that she was already suffering at the age she was baptised. It was a difficult reality to know that my parents had made baptismal vows they had already broken and continued to break. That realisation was sad. Feeling sad, I took Baby Girl out of the arms of Jesus and held her in my own arms and with that I felt Jesus putting his arms around all of us. In silence, we all promised we would care for Baby Girl and in turn we all imagined giving Baby Girl a kiss on her forehead. It was such a powerful moment – the sadness of what was before, merged with the happiness that we could do this differently now and provide the love, care and protection Baby Girl never had. And in the middle of that Jesus was holding all of us together, healing past wounds. All of that happening in the middle of a Sunday morning service that no one around me would have had any idea about. The sermon that day had been about solidarity – solidarity with each other and solidarity with God! The sermon mirrored all that had happened to us in that poignant moment. That day was the bringing together of the sadness for what was, and the happiness for what is now and what is ahead.

Sarah

As I got to know the various parts of Anna, I asked each part how best I could help them. I tried to be with them as I would any other small person especially a small person who was distressed or remembering something very painful. Sometimes it was about giving permission to scream or shout 'ow ow', as physical hurts surfaced. Sometimes the small person (and this was true not just with Anna) would say 'no no', 'go away' or 'stop it I don't like it'. I would allow the person to say whatever they needed to say and I would then repeat over and over again, 'yes you are allowed to shout or scream' but I would also remind them, 'this is now not then; this will never happen again. It is over.' It was about giving the person a different response to the trauma. Allowing the trauma to be expressed but at the same time ensuring that the new reality was shared with them.

Part of the healing is for the person to find ways to know and live in the NOW. Anna did it with her walks by the sea by repeating again and again that the abuse was no longer happening and saying the truth of who she was in God (loved, lovely, clever, kind etc.). In the early stages of her healing, Anna persisted in saying these truths to herself every day. It is hard to move from a repeating of the abuse in the memory to a place of it not happening now. I have encouraged adult parts to think about what can help their smaller parts to do that. For example, what would a treat look like for the different parts? A 6-year-old might want an ice cream; a 2-year-old might want to be snuggled up with a lovely story being read to her. Doing these things are so important to help the parts develop new memories within themselves.

Anna Girl usually wanted to write what she had remembered when she came to see me, and she learnt quickly that this helped her. She liked to use white paper and black felt tip for all the horrid words, memories and feelings and then she always wanted to take it to the bonfire in the garden and burn it. In the process of burning she found that she released the pain and memories to God. Afterwards she liked to have a pink piece of paper and would enjoy writing or drawing positive things such as 'I am lovely', 'I made some new amazing biscuits', 'Jesus really loves me', 'I am a very brave girl'. I encouraged Anna as I have others to stick this on the fridge or door so it can be read regularly. As Richard Rhor says:

> *'Be reminded that neuroscience now tells us that fear, negativity, and hatred stick like Velcro to the nerves, while positivity, gratitude, and appreciation slide away like Teflon from those same nerves — until we savor them, or choose them, for a minimum conscious fifteen seconds! Only then do they imprint! Please reflect on this. The positive, loving, and non-argumentative savoring of the moment is called contemplation.*[5]

Repeating the positive statements until they stick is an essential part of the healing from any kind of trauma where there has been fear or negativity. In abuse there is both.

Anna's healing happened because she understood her part in all this. She was prepared to take the time and responsibility to help herself with her journey of healing. She persisted even on the darkest of days to walk in the light and love, which she felt more easily on the joy-filled days. She persisted in telling all her parts that she would be there for them, that she loved them, and they could do life differently from now on.

I am reminded of the story of the paralysed man that is in three of the Gospels (Mark 2:1–12; Matthew 9:2–8; Luke 5:17–26).

Part of my work as Diocesan Advisor was to facilitate Christian healing days in different places around the diocese. One of the titles of these was 'Healing the paralysed parts of me'. Part of the morning session was to invite those attending to give responses to the different types of paralysis: physical, emotional and spiritual. These are some of the responses.

> *Physical paralysis – unmovable, trapped, stuck, bound, restricted, numb, lifeless, and helpless.*
>
> *Emotional paralysis – broken, fixed, can't cry, immune, mute, unable and restricted/constricted.*
>
> *Spiritual paralysis – frightened, the absence of God, confused, blind, fearful, isolated, disengaged, lost, despair and cut off.*

There is something in all these words that is true for the person who had been abused. In the conversations on the day people came to an understanding of their own places of paralysis. As the story from the Bible was studied in small groups there was an increased understanding that Jesus had healed all of the man. Yes he had healed him physically – he would not have been able to take up his mat and walk otherwise – but he had been healed relationally. He was restored to his friends and family and in meeting Jesus had been healed spiritually.

Anna's gradual integration and healing of her parts was a similar healing from paralysis. In the trauma she had been stuck in the places of fear, stuck in the lies and stuck in the memories. It was her healing from all that had paralysed her which enabled her process of integration.

Anna

Several months after the integration began to really embed within me, I stopped all contact with my parents. It was one of the most difficult points I reached, and I have described my process about that in a separate chapter in the book. But a week or so after I stopped all contact with my parents Anna Girl began telling me that 'the teenage part wants to tell her story one day'. I acknowledged what Anna Girl was saying and began to ponder it some more. Anna Girl had said for a long time that she was the oldest of the younger parts, but the more Anna Girl was learning to just be the 10-year-old she was, I realised there was probably a teenage part within me, but still hidden.

When Anna Girl spoke to Sarah not long after this, she said the same thing to her about the teenage part. Sarah said, 'I'll be ready to listen to her when she's ready to speak.' I realised at this point that this other part of me was lingering and about to emerge. It evoked all sorts of feelings inside me and there was a struggle going on within me for several days after seeing Sarah. I verbalised the struggle out loud to myself and God one evening. I felt it was Teenage Anna's struggle within me, about whether she wanted to emerge and if she also could be loved. So, in the struggle, I invited Teenage Anna to join us in the same way I had many months ago with the other little parts. I then experienced her absolute fear of having emerged after being hidden and split off for so long. In sensing her fear, I said to that part of me, 'I love you, it's safe here with us' and I repeated it over and over again to her.

So, there was now me – the adult and six little parts of me, fully integrated within me. No aspect of myself hidden any longer. There was another part to get used to and another part of myself to understand and learn all about. I realised how terrified the teenage part of me was the next day. I suddenly felt scared doing things that wouldn't usually make me fearful, such as getting dressed, undressed, taking a bath. I had to continue reassuring Teenage Anna that it was safe, and my father was no longer around. I knew that Teenage Anna had only emerged because I had just stopped contact with my parents. She was probably the part of me that was very afraid of my father. It's the part of me that became depressed in adolescence and withdrawn. Teenage Anna withdrew for a reason and it was for survival. As I was thinking about all this whilst driving somewhere, I had tears rolling down my face. If ever I needed confirmation of the most difficult decision I'd made (being the right one) to stop contact with my parents, this was it. Teenage Anna was a wonderful part of me that needed to belong within me, with all of me.

During the weeks that followed this, I was very busy with work, but I think the busyness allowed Teenage Anna to be within me, without any focus or pressure. Teenage Anna liked to watch and listen, and I think she needed that space. As time went on Teenage Anna began to experience that the way we were living now was very different to how she had lived as a teenager. She said something to Sarah about it being 'more free and not controlled', unlike how it had been living with my father. I began to realise how controlled I'd been as a teenager as her feelings and memories emerged within me.

Over time, as I lived with the parts of me being more integrated, I realised how significant it has been on my journey of recovering from abuse. I think one main aspect within the process was having Jesus at the heart of it. Having Jesus at the heart of the integration enabled parts of me to heal in ways I never imagined. For example, in my head, Jesus has been cradling Baby Girl in his arms alongside us and in doing that, the very small vulnerable infant within me that had been traumatised has become calmer, happier and is usually in absolute peace. It's a stark contrast to the screaming infant that I'd felt in pain and loneliness for as long as I could remember.

Jesus was the common thread that held all of me together again. When teenage Anna integrated inside me, she was very honest about her doubts about God, as I had been at that age. I remember so well the struggle Teenage Anna had about her faith when she emerged. She was consumed by fear and memories of how she had been hurt by our mother and father, almost as if she was still living it, in very much the same way the other parts had been until they starting letting go. On one particular day, whilst walking at the beach I spoke to Teenage Anna in my head about her struggle. As we walked along, I told her she had a choice, not like in the past when she had no choice, but now she could choose to do something differently. Teenage Anna knew that God had been helping all of me and I reminded her of the faith we had in Him and through Him we had new life. It was like throwing a lifeline to a desperate adolescent who was continually believing she was better off dead. Sadly, that thought pattern had become quite entrenched for the teenage part of me after suffering for such a prolonged period of time. I gently reminded Teenage Anna that she did not have to believe that any longer and there was in fact another way to live now which could free her from the pain of our mum and dad. Teenage Anna had never believed there was a way out and I knew that part of me desperately wanted to escape the pain she was in.

As we continued walking along, Teenage Anna said that she really wanted to try and do things another way. Internally I hugged her with Jesus for her bravery in wishing to do something different. So, we decided we would go to evensong later in the day so that we could share the choice she was making with God, in the place we honoured and where we felt safe. That day, Teenage Anna decided that there was a choice she had, which was to step out of the darkness and into the light. In the most beautiful way, Teenage Anna declared her faith in God that day at evensong when she said the words of the Creed aloud. As a teenager I had never said the words of services at church out loud because at that age I had given up hope in God. But on this day, she chose that she too wished to trust in God to help her out of the pain and into new life. I remember how significant that moment was in that every part of me shared my faith in God and trusted Him for all things. That decision had not come easily or lightly, it was with much heartache over many, many months. But when it happened, it was as if I was now being truly held together in one body, mind and spirit.

Teenage Anna shares with you an email that she wrote to Sarah the following day:

> *Sarah,*
>
> *I wrote down what happened in my book but I want to tell you now because it is a really big thing and it's made me cry this morning, but sort of happy crying I think, like a change crying.*
>
> *Anna said yesterday when we were at the beach that I didn't have to stay in the horrible place with all the lies and if I walked in the light with Jesus, instead, my dad wouldn't win like you said. I said I wanted to try because I understood what you were both saying and I didn't know there had been any other choice before but I wanted to get away from the lies.*
>
> *We went to evensong and I listened to all the singing and then I said the words with Anna for the first time – the creed. I have never said it before because I didn't know if I could believe and trust God and Jesus but I want to now – wow that's big isn't it???!! I want to know what it feels like to not be in the dark and all the lies where my mum and dad left me.*
>
> *When we drove to the airport this morning, Anna was praying and I asked to pray too and I talked to God and asked him to help me and I said I want to trust him and Jesus to help me and I want to hold Jesus' hand so I don't get lost.*
>
> *Me and Anna cried lots. I'm crying inside now writing this to you. Thank you for helping me Sarah. Will you help me understand things more and help me throw all the lies away to find out who I am?*
>
> *Lots of love from Teenage Anna xxx*

Sarah

My experience with Teenage Anna was one of taking things very slowly, of asking before we did anything and having a 'deal' with her that I would always tell her the truth. There had been so many lies for Teenage Anna and truth was very important to her. She always knew if others were lying to her. I also told her when she asked me complicated questions of faith and theology, 'this is what I think but there would be others who would have a completely different opinion'. She understood that there were things which I could only say, 'this is what I think, this is what I believe, but others will see it differently.' Teenage Anna asked me questions all the time about me, life, faith and God. She loved reading, so I would encourage her to read books as well as the Bible. Very early on as she was wanting to explore what faith meant for her, I gave her her own Youth Bible. I have found that if different parts have something of their own to read this can be very healing. It was a recognition that having the Bible in a format that would suit a teenager would help her. We discussed what she should read first and then she would put pencil marks all over the place and come with questions related to what she had been reading. This was challenging as some of her questions needed me to look things up in other books, but she enjoyed us discovering together. This is part of the building of a new relationship, about how to live well in the here and now. That ability was essential to Teenage Anna's healing and has also been with others I've been alongside. The challenge for me is to share the gospel, the love and healing of Jesus with each part in an appropriate way. Teenage Anna did and still does challenge my faith and my understanding. We often discuss and debate what she had read.

I have found that, for me, the person who is alongside needs to have the ability to listen to each part at a deep level. Each part may have a different voice or way of speaking. I have found that some parts are very wary, and they can find it difficult or even impossible to engage. Waiting for the right time and being consistent is important. It is crucial that I can be trustworthy to each part, not to be a person who says one thing and then does another, or not doing as I've agreed. It is fundamental that the parts know that this new relationship is safe and true.

In some cases, the parts are not aware of each other; with some people all the parts are aware of each other all the time. It is complicated and there is no standard of how it will be. I am more concerned with listening to whoever wanted to speak and trusted me enough. And in listening, enabling that part to know they are in the 'now' and that the conversation we're having is 'now' even if the memories are from years and years ago. Someone I was working with was very surprised when I encouraged them to look at my diary and they realised it was 2015, not 1985. Their memory was from 1985, but the part thought it was happening now, in 2015. Until that moment that part had only existed in what happened to them then. It is the reason that they coped with the trauma by becoming a dissociated part. It is often the realisation for the part that someone is actually listening to them which is so important. It is not because of what they 'do' but because someone is interested in their life, their experiences and is not going to hurt them. In a way, it is like the way God relates to us. We often get caught into the 'doing' as Christians, to try and 'prove' our worth to God. But in Jesus we see that he just loved to be with us, spending time getting to know those who wanted to be with him.

I have often loved parts of people long before the adult person has done so, as Anna identified. And in doing so it enabled Anna to learn how to love those parts for herself. But for some people even acknowledging they have parts is difficult. It means they have to face the truth of all that was done to them. It also means that they may need help acknowledging they have dissociated parts and perhaps even saying thank you to them. I always say thank you to the part for sharing. It is this that Anna was able to watch and then model for herself. If people choose to deny their parts, it is much harder for there to be any healing. The more they can love their parts and allow Jesus to love them too, the greater the possibility of healing.

Carolyn Spring[d] has produced some excellent workshops and material both about trauma and the neuroscience of dissociation.

In learning to understand the response to trauma, it is about finding ways for people to alter their responses now that they are no longer in the trauma. This process of self-understanding is part of the healing. All this can be achieved with a trauma therapist who has a good understanding of dissociation. Anna had done some of this in therapy before I met her. The difference in the encounters I have with people is that I expect the spiritual part of the person to engage as well. Prayer is a key part of their healing both being prayed for but much more having and establishing a rhythm of prayer for themselves.

In some Christian churches, where there is a lack of understanding of both trauma and dissociation, I have seen how Christians have seen the part of someone as a 'demon'. This is wrong. It shows a complete lack of understanding of both trauma and what happens in the brain following trauma. It is a stark refusal to understand the proven neuroscience of the person and if any kind of deliverance ministry is carried out in such circumstances it perpetuates the abuse and retraumatises the individual. Loving and listening to parts as loving and listening to any individual is the place of healing. Jesus came and brought healing and very often that was by meeting the whole person, listening to their reply to his question of 'What do you want me to do for you?' It is a question I too ask people especially when they first come to see me. Perhaps because of the years of therapy and then her newfound faith Anna was able to share what she wanted and also trust me to listen to her parts. She eventually started to listen to them as well.

Some people find having a book that parts write in really helpful. They can share what they are feeling, how they could be helped, or what they want to do today. If the adult part can commit to reading that, writing back and responding, things start to change. A conversation develops and each person has to find their own way of doing things. Anna found this worked for her, but others have found other ways. The important thing is to commit to trying to understand and have a conversation. With that openness come all sorts of possibilities for healing.

As Carolyn Spring[d] suggests in her work, anything that helps to ground the person at the time of fear or panic will help to shift the response. To help shift the focus from the trauma response, I have suggested to people they may want to engage in an activity such as doing a puzzle, or writing, singing, listening to music, prayer, going for a walk or doing some physical exercise. Encouraging the person to notice what is happening is what Anna describes clearly. This encourages the person to be curious as to what is going on... 'I feel anxious now because…' This is the 'just notice' moment which then enables the person to shift their focus which can help them to reach out and connect, such as asking themselves what would Sarah think, let me write to Sarah, let me phone someone and speak to them. It all helps to break the freeze response and develop new, healthier patterns of coping.

Anna

Once I had integrated all the parts within me, I spent time getting to know me all over again. I had now learnt to listen to myself in a way I had never done before and to help myself in a more nurturing and respectful way. In the early days of integrating I was fragile and had to take really good care of myself. If we couldn't do something one day, we didn't do it. If we needed to sleep, we slept. If 6-year-old Anna needed to write or draw, she did. If Anna Girl needed to email Sarah, she did. There was something different I experienced in this than all the years I had been in therapy. Therapy has very tight boundaries around it, which I completely understand and respect. But the tightness of those boundaries did not allow for the freedom of recovery that I was now experiencing. In the tightness of boundaries in the past, I had probably constrained my ability to just 'go with the flow'. In learning to really nurture myself as Sarah was doing with me, I had to learn that in this stage of the process it was OK to do the things I needed to do. I still had to work, so there were some things in my day that had to be done, but I learnt to pace myself. I didn't book in work after seeing Sarah because I knew we would be exhausted, and we kept Sundays for worshipping at the cathedral and not doing much else. On days off, I rested. And in *really* nurturing and caring for myself, for all of me, I could feel patterns shifting inside me. That may sound odd, but I could feel subtle changes. I had lived under constant fear and pressure as a child, so in fact I'd never learnt to relax. Learning to rest and relax now took practice, but I began to feel myself accept that it was a good thing.

There was also something else that I really noticed as my past traumas of abuse were healing; and that was something about self-regulation. There has been much written about the impact of trauma and poor attachments on children's capacity to self-regulate their emotions. This is due to the poor or negligent interactions they have received which prevent that capacity developing within the brain. In my personal experience, I had grown up always on high alert, probably with high levels of stress due to fear or panic. And I had grown up with no adult being able to consistently help me manage and understand my feelings. So, my feelings were either shut off or at times were overwhelming me. And those patterns continued into adulthood. Therapy began to help me understand my feelings in a better way. But something more dramatically shifted in my ability to self-regulate once I had integrated every part of myself within me. From learning to understand each part of me that had become integrated, I have learnt what worries different parts of me, what scares me, what makes me happy and what triggers memories. And in doing that, when I experience the feelings of different parts of me, I know which part of me is struggling and then I know how to help myself. It was as if I had learnt to parent myself. Reassurance was a huge part of what I, as the adult, and Sarah had had to do with each little part – to know they are loved, to know they are safe, to know it's OK to feel, and to know it's OK to talk. So, each time I reassured parts of me, I developed a capacity to self-regulate instead of repeating the patterns of trauma, panic, stress and fear.

I have felt these changes so intrinsically inside me, it's hard to describe. And at the heart of that has been compassion and love. That's where I believe the combined spiritual and therapeutic work has enabled the healing to take place. They weren't split off parts any longer, they were little beings inside of me, different parts of me, but we are one whole person. If the adult part doesn't fully integrate with those parts, I can see that it would be impossible to show the other parts of yourself how much they are loved and how to help them experience the newness of life without abuse. For me, it has been like parenting five traumatised children within me, into a place of freedom – emotionally and spiritually.

Chapter 6
Beating in Time with the Heartbeat of God

Sarah

In this chapter Anna shares how time is managed as healing begins and about what it means to wait on God and the right time to proceed. Just as it takes time for a bone that is broken to heal, so too with any other healing.

Anna

> *But do not forget one thing, dear friends: to the Lord one day is a thousand years, and a thousand years is one day*
>
> *(2 Peter 3:8–9 Youth Bible).*

Sarah and I had many conversations about timings, including a conversation about '*How can we explain this in the book*?' Different parts of me also experienced timings in different ways, as you would expect of children at different ages.

Timings weren't just about the length of time though; there was something significant I learnt about when it seemed right to take a step in a certain direction, when to wait, when to act, when to rest. Resting was something I realised I had to relearn. I found I needed to learn to rest in a whole new way and *allow* myself to rest. I lay in bed one morning with my whole body aching, my mind so tired I did not want to do a thing. As I lay there, I was reminded of something I had listened to about surrender a couple of months previously. It was an analogy of allowing yourself to float in the water rather than fighting if you feel like you're sinking. It resonated with me and I realised that in resting I had to allow myself to rest in Jesus, rest in the exhaustion rather than fighting it. And in doing so the exhaustion somehow began to feel less debilitating. The 'resting in' Jesus sort of allowed me to feel freer in the exhaustion. I knew I needed to rest for the healing to take place, but it didn't mean that in resting I was defeated or disabled. It felt like I could rest inside myself and let Jesus rest with me. In this new space I knew that it was finally safe to rest without feeling like a failure and in fact resting would be my strength.

I'm not the most patient of people and I'm not sure many of us are. I had spent a lot of my adult life working in an environment where everybody wanted everything yesterday and it was a constant pressure of making decision after decision. The stress of that was immense, but it was probably my early experience of trauma that enabled my mind and body to deal with that level of stress every day. Physiologically my brain had been programmed to stress so it was the 'norm'. But when I stopped my professional work, I began to experience a different momentum. When I stopped, I was left only with myself and for the first time in my life I had only me to focus on. I found that was also true in the healing – I had to focus on myself. It wasn't comfortable at all. With my impatience I often wanted to know the answer or know the next step. But, over time, I began to realise that my relationship with God did not work in that way. Firstly, God gave us free will, so in fact he left me to make choices but, secondly, his timing was not always mine.

In surrendering my life to God, it was not a case of sitting back and waiting for God to act. It was about doing this with God instead of doing it alone. It was hard when I had only relied on myself as a way to survive. I realise now, looking back at the journey that at the beginning it was about me getting to know God and how He communicated to me because it's different for everyone. In the early part of this journey, it was as if God needed to show me that He was there and that I could rely on Him – perhaps like a young child constantly needing the reassurance from a parent. It reminds me of the story where Jesus talked to His disciples about the good shepherd: 'I am the good shepherd. I know my own and my own know me, just as the Father knows me and I know the

Father'. (John 10:14–15). Later on when Jesus is questioned by the Jews about whether he is the Messiah, he again refers to the good shepherd saying 'My sheep hear my voice. I know them, and they follow me' (John 10:27). In my relationship with Jesus, I felt as if I was continually learning to discern his 'voice', not a spoken voice that I can understand humanly, but a spiritual voice within my soul. And to listen at that level required time, patience, prayer and a willingness to continue opening my heart to God.

Quite often, it was during my walks by the sea that I felt God revealed things to me, spoke to me. The walks by the sea had become a daily rhythm of prayer, chatting to God in my head as I walked along. It was a space that I created for myself which became important. During those walks I found that suddenly something would make sense, or I would understand something and then more often than not I would then email Sarah telling her what the revelation was and what I needed to do next. And in the writing of the email, the clarity in the revelation happened. At the beginning of this journey, things could often be revealed several times within the space of a few days in between seeing Sarah. I'm not sure how Sarah kept up with the pace at that stage – she often described herself as running to catch up! And I became oblivious of the speed at the time until there was a bit of a break and I found myself sitting at the beach and realising I'd 'landed' in another place on the journey, not having realised how far I'd come.

There were also moments during those walks by the sea that I had a chance to reflect or just express my tiredness or sadness to Jesus. In the tiredness I enjoyed looking at the expanse of the sea. There is something about the energy of the sea that is beyond human control; it has a life of its own. It is a good reminder of God's creation, the wonder of God's creation. Those moments to connect with God's creation were important for me, because they allowed me to have a sense of the enormity of God's love. It also felt like a heaven and earth connection. I can't explain it but it was an opportunity to feel something of the divine, something beyond the difficulties of the world. That glimpse of an eternal perspective was like being given strength for the journey.

Sarah

Anna got in touch with The Living Well because she was specifically looking for a Christian healing centre. She found me on the Internet, and we arranged the first meeting by email. I was quite clear that God was part of the 'package' as we embarked on the healing journey. And within that I encouraged Anna to pray, to find somewhere to worship and to share what she was experiencing in that worship. I would pray for Anna, not just when we were together but every day for her and specifically in some situations and on some days when things were very tough. This was not, however, a one-way relationship. I hoped that she would pray for me and did ask sometimes for her to pray for something that I was involved in. This is one of those dynamics that alters everything. It is a mutual relationship. I too am on a journey of faith, a different one, but I also face days that are a great trial, I am still in need of fellowship and very much in need of prayer.

I believe that the questions that need to be considered by anyone if they are going to beat in time with the heartbeat of God are: do I have the time, space and a place to be able to listen to that heartbeat? The difference between what Anna and I did together, compared to the therapy Anna had previously engaged in, was that it was not just two of us on a journey but three. Jesus was there in the centre of it all. He was the one bringing the healing, showing the next step, guiding, loving and being.

Anna started worshipping at the cathedral. This was a good space for her because it had the sense of anonymity about it and less of a 'family' church feeling which was very important to her. For others, a smaller church may work better but, as discussed in a previous chapter, finding a place of worship if you have been abused within the church can be much harder. This is something that I always consider carefully with each person. As Anna found a place to worship regularly it helped us both because it gave a different backdrop to the whole process. It gave us a place to talk from, about what happened at the cathedral on Sunday and I would often hear the reflections from different perspectives; for example, 6-year-old Anna would not have experienced it in the same as the others. The differing perspectives were fascinating to hear. I was able to share some of the Bible stories of healing with Anna and we would sometimes pray into that. Sometimes God answered prayers before we had even really prayed them! And in doing so we laughed and gave thanks. When it took longer, we shared in the ongoing faithfulness of continuing to pray.

I never have any idea how long the healing process in situations like this will take. In emotional relational healing there is always a sense of loss. There are usually similar stages of a healing journey to that, such as grief, but the order of those stages cannot be fixed and the length of time for any one person is never known.

The process was about me and Anna trusting in God's timing and listening to the process for both of us. Over time, Anna learnt to trust that when she was overwhelmed with feelings, she would need time to be with those feelings, to just let them be. One of the things that Anna learnt was not to 'fight' against the feelings. It took time and trust in God to ensure she did not get overwhelmed by feelings. For example, Anna learnt that if she felt overwhelmed with body memories she needed to make time to rest and recover, to eat well and find something to do that would relax her, such as watching a film. It reminds me of how God knows what we need and times of rest and relaxation, food, water and sleep are all important. There is a story in the Bible (1 Kings 19:4–8) where God looks after a prophet called Elijah. Elijah had had enough, and he decides to sit down and allow death to overcome him. God, however, has other ideas and sends his angels to both feed and sustain him.

But [Elijah] went a day's journey into the wilderness, and came and sat down under a solitary broom tree. He asked that he might die: 'It

> *is enough; now, O Lord, take away my life, for I am no better than my ancestors.' Then he lay down under the broom tree and fell asleep. Suddenly an angel touched him and said to him, 'Get up and eat.' He looked, and there at his head was a cake baked on hot stones, and a jar of water. He ate and drank, and lay down again. The angel of the Lord came a second time, touched him, and said, 'Get up and eat, otherwise the journey will be too much for you.' He got up, and ate and drank; then he went in the strength of that food forty days and forty nights to Horeb the mount of God.*

With most people I work with, there comes a time when it feels like it is an impossible journey. The holding onto the light of Christ and believing in the positive statements just cannot be done. 'I can't go on like this', is how people often feel. My response is to encourage the person and enable them to get through the next five minutes rather than thinking about the whole day, which can feel overwhelming. Being reminded of how far they have come can help, as well as knowing that others have struggled and yet continued. Just as God sent an angel to Elijah to encourage him to rest and eat, it is really important that we also look after ourselves physically and emotionally. The journey of healing requires energy, so it is important to have times to rest and recover.

I often remind the person of some of the positive phrases that help them, such as 'Please, Jesus, be with me', 'Light always overcomes darkness', 'Jesus is my comforter' and 'I am wrapped in the duvet of God's love.' I pray for the person in as deep and real a way as I can – how best to help varies from person to person. Some may need encouragement and others may need more practical help, such as a cooked meal. Others need reminding that God and I are not giving up on them, so I ask them to consider whether they really want to give up on themselves. I often suggest that they light a candle and claim the light of Christ, listen to worship music and read the Bible. These practical things can help the person to shift the focus from the awfulness they feel. Self-harm and suicide attempts are a real possibility, but I know that God can and does send his angels to minister to us at such times. I have to hold onto faith in God and His ministry, as Michael Mitton explains:

> *'On the journey, we are sustained by the angels, those signs of heaven breaking in, who release to us the power of God. Most crucially, we are sustained by the knowledge that only the Spirit can give, that we, struggling mortals, are held secure in the all-embracing love of Father, Son and Holy Spirit. Such knowledge does not provide slick and easy answers, but it does give us a home in which to dwell, wherein we can know the company of the wounded Lamb of God. In such company all of us may offer and receive the compassionate, gentle and powerful healing grace of God.'*
>
> *(Michael Mitton).*[7]

What is essential for the journey is helping people to know something of the presence of God and that He will sustain them as they continue on.

It is a time of understanding when to surrender and allow yourself to go with the waiting, because resisting will not work. The process cannot be hurried. For example, Anna had to allow the body memories to be felt as they happened; they had been pushed away for so long. And in allowing those pains to come out, especially for the younger parts of her, the pain could for the first time in her life be healed. She at times felt battered from the torrent of memories, not unlike being in the torrent of a fast-flowing river. But as she let herself go with the flow of the river, she began to reach places of stillness, like a still pool at the side of a river where she could rest and allow those memories to be healed. In not resisting that process the power of the memories and the pain subsided. In the same way emotional feelings are remembered, the body also remembers and, in remembering, the pain is felt afresh. (Peter A Levine, *Waking the Tiger* and Bessel Van Der Kolk *The Body Keeps the Score*)

This is a new way of being for anyone who has been abused, because it has been the fight and freeze that has kept the person alive. And in the healing, they have to do this bit differently. They have to enter into it rather than run away from it or resist it. It is also about learning who the person can rely on; as Anna says, she had to learn to rely on God in new ways. Jesus' life helps to teach us about both relying on God and understanding the difficulty of the journey.

Chapter 7
Letting Go

Sarah

In this chapter Anna shares how she gradually let go of the abuse and the relationships that were a key part of her life.

Anna

I've thought a lot about why and how I arrived at a place of wishing to 'let go'. People talk a lot about 'letting go'. I remember the first time I told someone about the abuse. The first reaction of that person and many people subsequently were, 'put it in the past now, let go and move on'. I remember how angry I used to feel when people said that and somehow made an assumption that it was that easy to do! I had suffered years of trauma and suddenly people were saying 'let go and move on'. Believe me, it wasn't that I didn't want to let go and move on, but it sort of felt disrespectful when people said that phrase and left me quite confused. I had wanted to scream 'Don't you know how awful this has been?' Saying 'let go and move on' felt like my parents, my abusers saying to me 'I don't know why you're so unhappy, just get on'. So, the phrase 'let go and move on' seemed to add fuel to my already confused mind. From my experience, letting go isn't straightforward and anyone hearing a survivor's story of abuse needs to think carefully before responding with a phrase such as 'let go and put it behind you'.

For me, the confusion about being told to just 'move on' was that I firstly needed to have a sense that I was believed, and I felt I needed to talk through the horrors of what I'd suffered. The moment from first telling someone that I'd been abused to the moment of feeling ready to 'let go' was a very long process: many, many years. To be honest, I didn't actually think it was possible to let go. I don't think I even knew what letting go meant. How do you let go? What happens? How does it go? They were all questions

I'd had. And I hadn't found those answers until I began to bring faith into my recovery. Up until then it had just seemed the greatest mystery; everyone advising it was the best thing to do but no one had ever been able to help me know how. So, I had just left it at that and assumed that I wasn't perhaps brave enough to let go. The thought that I wasn't brave enough sat alongside the thoughts that I was horrible and stupid, and it remained there.

Until, that is, I found my faith in God and began to realise that the collection of thoughts I'd held about myself all my life were not in fact true and did not belong to me. How did these things change when I brought faith into my recovery? I think as I began to think about things spiritually, I started to feel hopeful about letting go. In the early stages of finding my faith in God I read a lot about forgiveness. I don't like using the word too much as it can get misinterpreted by people, as I too had misinterpreted it. I am also conscious that forgiveness can be used in quite abusive ways to survivors of abuse by some Christians saying things such as 'if you don't forgive you won't be forgiven'. Saying things like that without a survivor fully understanding the theology behind the statement or what that phrase means can lead survivors of abuse to run as far away from God as possible. There seemed a lot of power associated with *needing* to forgive in some of the things I read, and I struggled with it. Thankfully it didn't turn me away from God; it made me want to understand Him better. I knew that there was something about forgiveness and its true meaning that held another key to my freedom and that sense of knowing made me determined to work it out with God.

What I began to understand and from some helpful conversations with a few people in the church, the volunteers at Life Centre[a] and later with Sarah was that forgiveness didn't mean anything about accepting or forgetting the abuse. It didn't even mean anything about the other person or about needing to have a relationship with them or telling them I had forgiven them. I realised it was about a choice. It was about saying 'I don't want to carry this anymore and

I want to hand this to God'. In essence, it felt to me like 'letting go'. Prior to this I had assumed forgiveness meant accepting what my parents had done and, in some ways, giving power back to them and saying, 'it's OK what you've done to me'. Beginning to understand my assumptions were wrong, compared to my new understanding of God's meaning of forgiveness, gave me a different perspective.

I read more and talked to Sarah more about forgiveness. My trust in God had been growing and I think that was important for me in the process of letting go. I started to feel the enormity of the choice to let go. But I gradually started to understand that if I made a choice to give the abuse and my parents to God and hand it over to Him, saying, 'this is for you to deal with now', it would no longer be my responsibility. When I began to think about that I began to see how responsible I'd felt, carrying the abuse for my whole life. Suddenly being aware how responsible I'd felt was a significant realisation. The abuse and my parents had felt like my responsibility to keep safe and keep secret, my responsibility to know what to do with it/them, whether to have an ongoing relationship with them, whether to confront them... the list was endless. I suddenly realised how responsible I'd been feeling and that I'd carried that responsibility forever. I could then see how abusive that was. What they had done to me had never been my responsibility but somehow right within the abuse it had been passed to me along with the pain, the hurt and the false identity of myself.

So, I pondered.... If I gave it to God what would He do with it? I wasn't really sure, but I did know He was ultimately the one being who could deal with it. God is a God of forgiveness, and what He did with it would be His decision, not mine. I wasn't sure how I felt about that. I realised I was so used to being in control of all this. I thought about how I would feel if God forgave them, that maybe God hadn't realised how bad it had been if He forgave them. I think I actually wanted Him to punish them and make them suffer. Somehow, I didn't like the thought of my parents being 'let off the hook', so to speak. I thought that God would surely want them to suffer in some way for the acts of abuse they had carried out on me. I perhaps wanted God to do what any loving parent would feel like doing if they found out their child was being abused by someone. But the fundamental part of giving this to God was understanding that God isn't human; he doesn't think and act as humans do. God is God. 'God said to Moses, "I am who I am"' (Exodus 3:14). God doesn't think as we think; His thinking is beyond our understanding. That's part of the mystery of God!

So I debated all this in my head for some time until I sort of came full circle again to understanding the truth about God. There may be a huge theological debate about whether God punishes which I wouldn't be able to explain. But it was one of the first questions I asked Sarah when I met her – 'Does God punish?' At that time, I was asking from the perspective that maybe God was punishing me and that's why things had gone wrong in my life. Sarah's answer to the question stuck with me. She said she didn't believe He did and explained that, if He did, it would be a little bit like God holding us all as puppets on a string that He controlled, and God didn't really work like that. This was Sarah's perspective. She did say that there were always consequences to our actions, but she didn't believe it was about God punishing.

Sarah's response not only helped me to think about myself and the questions I'd had about whether I was being punished but it also fed into the growing debate in my head about letting go and forgiveness. If God didn't punish me (and I believe he doesn't), it meant He doesn't punish others either. And if this isn't about punishment, what did it leave me with then? Back to the beginning I came again, to the original questions about truth; who was God and what was He about? In my growing faith and relationship with God, I was beginning to feel that God was about love and peace and hope. But God was also about justice. I mulled all this over for some time. I kept talking to people about forgiveness and I kept saying 'I'm not ready yet'. And that was OK. But inside I was starting to feel ready to let go.

When I had a significant moment of realising how damaging holding onto the abuse was for me as I sat on the beach talking to God, I decided that there was no way that I could continue re-experiencing the abuse internally, through the memories. I needed to start letting go and allowing myself to be free like I'd never been as an infant or child. At that moment, it was as if Jesus had scooped me up in his loving arms and said to all of me 'you don't have to feel abused anymore'. The choice to let go now made complete sense! If I could let go, I could stop the memories of the abuse from persistently re-traumatising me.

The two things – letting go and forgiveness – now seemed much the same thing. Knowing that I wanted to let go, that I needed to, in fact, I embarked on the next stage of the journey with Sarah. For the first time in my life I had a growing sense of what it meant to let go and how I was going to do it. I knew I needed to 'give to God'. During times with Sarah of remembering the abuse, she had often prayed for Jesus to take the memories from me, so I was perhaps already gaining a sense of him being able to hold things with me through her prayers. But I knew I needed to do something more symbolic, something that would really allow me to have a sense of letting go and giving to God.

I turned up to see Sarah on one occasion and asked for pens and paper, knowing that I needed to write a letter to God. I had decided that I wanted to first let go of the lies, the false things I'd understood about who I was and the lies my parents had told me. So that's what I did. I wrote down all the words I had falsely believed about myself – I'm stupid, I'm horrible... all those and many more that I now knew were lies. When I finished, Sarah took me into the chapel where she prayed with me as I clutched the letter. We then walked out to the garden to the bonfire and I asked Sarah to burn it. As she did, I knew in my heart that I'd let go of the lies to God. I had actively chosen to release them from me and lifted them to God. It was a beautifully sunny day in the garden and, after letting go, I then did some more writing with Sarah in the garden but this time I wrote down all the words about the truth of who I am 'I am loved, I am lovely, I am loveable, I am clever, I know the truth, I am brave and I am free'. I symbolically replaced all that I gave to God, with the truth of who I now was in God. That day was the first day I realised letting go was possible.

How did it feel after that? I had a sense that I had given the lies about myself to God. The significance of writing down the truth about myself was important. It sort of left me with something to hold on to instead. But it then took a daily dedication of saying the words about who I was, to myself. Every day that I sat down at the beach I said them in my head to God or, if it was quiet, aloud to God. It was difficult. For years I had said to myself I was horrible and stupid and now I was saying I was lovely and loveable! It wasn't easy to do at first, but I persisted through the uncomfortableness every day. As the days and weeks passed, the words began to sink further and further into me and it began to feel less uncomfortable and more true. If I had a bad day, the lies would creep back into my thought pattern, but what helped me was to sit with the writing and read those new words about myself aloud. It helped to shift the lies, which was incredibly powerful.

As time went on, the notion of letting go and forgiving became much deeper and more profound. By taking this initial step of letting go of the lies, I felt ready to start letting go of other things. In recalling painful memories about the abuse, part of the process with Sarah became about different parts of me writing down what we wanted to give to God from the memories and off to the bonfire we went to burn it. The more I did that, the more I felt like I was shedding the lies and the abuse from within me and I gradually began to feel freer to find the Anna that God created and to feel freer to be myself.

Giving the memories to God wasn't about eradicating them from me. What had happened to me was part of my life and those memories will always be within me. But I gave the pain of them to God, the awfulness of what I'd experienced physically and emotionally. Over time, by giving the pain of the memories to God, that pain I had always felt in my core did begin to shift. It came through a combination of letting go, learning to love myself and taking care of myself. Every now and then memories continue to resurface, but when they do, they now don't consume me in the way they had. That feels miraculous!

Over time, working through this with Sarah and giving more and more of the abusive memories to God, I began to feel that I was ready to give my relationship with my parents to God. I think this is when I truly felt ready to forgive. I began to realise that letting go meant freeing myself and no longer holding on to things that God could take for me. I realised that ultimately God would be the judge of my parents, not me; and if I gave them to God then He could lift that heavy burden of responsibility from me. I could pass them to God with all the pain they had caused me.

I firstly forgave my mother. I did this by praying to God over a period of time that I wasn't responsible for her anymore and I began to pray that God would help her to find a better way. This truly felt like the beginnings of forgiveness and felt right. I had felt so responsible for my mother whilst growing up; to make her better or happier, to protect her, care for her, shield her from the truth. All sorts of ways. But in handing her to God, I was asking God to help her instead of me helping her. I was asking God to take the burden of all she had done to me. I began to understand that God could indeed forgive both my parents, but it was actually for my parents to seek that forgiveness from God. They would ultimately have to turn to Him and that wasn't for me to worry about. As time went on, I began to pray for my dad too. I gave him to God and said, 'Please God help him to find a better way.' I prayed that both my parents could find God and be changed. For me this was the ultimate letting go of my parents and freed me to really break away from them emotionally and spiritually in the way I needed to, in order to continue the journey.

It wasn't a magical moment when suddenly everything was OK after I forgave them; it was just part of the process. And in fact, it's a continual process. There are times that I repeat these prayers to God, particularly at significant times in the year or if they have been in my head a lot. But doing that enables me, each time, to just lift them from me to God. It's almost like taking the suffocating cloak of abuse off me and passing it to God. I didn't need to continue feeling suffocated by it.

There was a lot more letting go, in so many other ways which happened after this. It seemed to be the transforming part of the journey because, the more I walked in the truth, anything that wasn't truth or didn't seem right inside me anymore had to go. Not all at once – it was a process. I never had a plan of what to let go of next, I just took each step and dealt with whatever God faced me with next. The weird thing to experience was that in many areas of my life, things that had seemed so significant and important no longer were. Sometimes I felt like I was seeing my world and the world before me through new eyes.

Sometimes there were things that I wasn't even aware that I needed to let go of! One of these particular things related to a feeling of loneliness. It was a feeling that had always been around, but there was a period of a few weeks where it felt like the loneliness just got a real hold of me and I began trying to make sense of where it was coming from, what it was really about. I had been away working for a weekend and found myself alone in a different city with some time on my hands. I had spent some time exploring. On one level that was lovely in the new freer state I was finding myself in, but the feeling of loneliness just kept creeping in. Everywhere I looked I saw families and couples and friends; I couldn't see another lone person like me. The feelings of wanting a family of my own, a partner, was all I could think about. This had been my wish every night as a child. That evening as I sat in a hotel room the loneliness swarmed me again. But as I sat with it, I realised it was demobilising me, keeping me stuck. I then began to realise that the loneliness was about my old expectations of what should have been, the things I had wanted in my life. But in finding my faith in God, I was now walking a new path. Therefore, if I kept hold of the 'should have beens' I would not be able to embrace where I was. I realised I no longer had control over what the future was to be and I certainly didn't want to take control and try and create old expectations. I could only walk the path I found myself on. I decided that night I needed to let go of those old wishes and expectations too. That was hard, but it felt necessary.

A few days later this verse came to me while listening to a daily prayer:

> *'I am the true vine, and my Father is the vinegrower. He removes every branch in me that bears no fruit. Every branch that bears fruit he prunes to make it bear more fruit'*
>
> *(John 15:1–2).*

It really helped me to understand a little more about letting go and the loneliness that I had been feeling, perhaps as a result of having started to free myself of so many things. I had let go of lots in a short space of time. I'd let go of memories, feelings, ambitions, control, people and much, much more. But as this verse so vividly describes, each of these branches had needed to be cut off or pruned within me, and it was no wonder I was feeling so bare, so alone and vulnerable. But I now lived in hope of the new branches and fruit I could bear because of that. It was an uncomfortable place to be because it was so unknown but I had to keep trusting in God.

I also listened to a sermon on Trinity Sunday that helped me. It spoke of how to consider the Trinity (Father, Son and Holy Spirit) through an analogy of a garden. The sermon described that you can't look at a garden from the outside; you actually have to step inside to see its full beauty. But at the time it made me think about the other parts of being within a garden; and that it needs to be constantly tended to, pruned and cut back in order to continue to see its full beauty. But you also can't start pruning until you step inside. In terms of the Trinity, I had needed to step into my relationship with Father, Son and Holy Spirit. I needed the Holy Spirit to enable me to find my way and continually discern what needed to go, what was truth and what could remain. The Holy Spirit had, over the months, been helping me create my internal garden, now built in the love of God. It wasn't perhaps the way I'd imagined or how I'd thought it would look. But that was what was different about letting go of my life and allowing the unexpected to happen, however difficult. Jesus talks about faith coming at huge cost, having to walk paths that seem impossible and at times feeling lonely. I felt that. But I was also beginning to experience a little of the beauty and freedom I was creating with God and I knew that ultimately God, within the Trinity, would continue to fill my garden with hope.

Sarah

I think forgiveness is one of the hardest things that we do in life. It means that the very depths of ourselves have to come to terms with a person and situation that has caused us harm, agony and grief.

In my view, forgiveness is a continual process. It begins with the question of 'Can I believe in a God who forgives?' For me, Jesus' life and work on the cross means I do believe in a God of forgiveness. Sometimes, believing in that is all that I or others are able to do. In doing so, they can stay in a place of believing that God forgives but also that God accepts if the person, at any given time, doesn't feel able to forgive. It is still God's work and the person can leave the situation or person in God's hands. Sometimes, later on, the person may want to do a bit more. They often begin to wonder how their belief in a God of forgiveness leads them to live in that stream of God's will, God's Holy Spirit. The person starts to live in the truth of the God who does forgive, and they then begin to question whether they can also forgive.

People sometimes reach a point whereby they no longer want the person or situation in their head and no longer want to continue stoking up the fire of hatred and disgust that they may feel about them. And in reaching this point, they begin to feel that they want to let go. In letting go, we then leave the situation or person in God's hands which leaves God to deal with it, even if that involves God's forgiveness. This can be a very difficult decision to make as Anna has described. We long to forgive because we stand in the truth of forgiveness but somehow our humanness can find it hard to believe a God who can forgive the most awful of things that people have done to one another. But if we stand in the truth of our God who does forgive, over time, we begin to realise it is right to hand the person or situation to God. Instead of trying to do God's work for Him, we let Him in to it instead. We allow God into our pain caused by another and ask Him to do His work, to both set us free and to set the other person free. When someone reaches this point, they find that when the person who hurt them comes into their mind, they have a choice; to stoke up the feelings of hatred and pain or to say 'you are in God's hands now, so out of my head you go'.

This is not easy and is one of the most difficult things we can do. It takes practice but I have found in my work with others that there are practical things that can help. Burning paper with pictures, words or memories is often very helpful for people. I have a special container for burning paper so that it does not blow away and the person can watch it burn in front of them. The fire can feel cleansing and often people feel that what they have burnt has been lifted to God. I also have a paper shredder which other people prefer to use. I never expect the person to forgive and I always leave people to make their own choices in their own time. God will help the person in their own time and in their own way, it is not for me to dictate another's process. I always hope that others will believe that God can forgive even if they cannot and, in believing this, that they will no longer have the pain that has had a hold on them for so long. This is all part of someone's healing and taking control of a situation where they had no control.

I have found over the years that many people are able to move from the initial stage of forgiveness to greater depths of forgiveness over time. I have often heard stories from survivors of abuse who have been told by clergy that the first thing they must do is forgive. This seemingly cold, bald statement so often said, when survivors may not even be able to think about that, can be so unhelpful. Some survivors have been told by others in the church that they will not be healed unless they forgive. This can feel very abusive. It is not of our will, but of God's alone. A survivor of abuse has already often felt very shamed in their experiences and for another person to insinuate that healing is dependent on the survivor's ability to forgive is the most unhelpful pastoral advice that can be given. Jesus forgave from the cross with no conditions and he can and does the same today.

What can be extremely helpful for survivors of abuse is to be left in their own stream of forgiveness, to have someone to walk alongside them and be there to answer questions and support them, if and when they want to understand more about letting go. I often say to those I am privileged to walk with, forgiveness is so very hard. I need to believe that God is a better justice maker than I am. I need His forgiveness for me for all that I have done wrong and so I also need to leave others with Him who need forgiveness. Sometimes people who find they are able to let go explain to me that it begins to feel different for them, that they find the abusive person or memory is no longer continually in their head. Some reach a point on the journey when they say to me, 'I may one day be able to forgive them'. Wow! That is a moment of grace that has integrity and honesty. We all have to be honest about our capacity to forgive and know that whatever we feel unable or able to do is right for us at that time.

The story Jesus told in the parable of the prodigal son helps us to look at what happens in the process of forgiveness. The story not only shows us God's warm, open, welcoming arms, waiting for the person needing forgiveness, but it also shows, through the eyes of the brother, how hard it is for us as humans to comprehend the father who so willingly forgives. The brother thinks 'but why have you not punished him for all he did wrong?' The father's response to the son who had gone astray is to give him the best clothes and to organise the finest feast saying to the angry brother, 'Son, you are always with me, and all that is mine is yours. But we had to celebrate and rejoice, because this brother of yours was dead and has come to life; he was lost and has been found.' (Luke 15: 31–32).

Anna Girl wrote me a poignant message one day after she had told me the pain she was in from experiencing memories. I had said to her that I'd been upset she was in so much pain and needed her prayers for me to be more forgiving of her father. She said to me

> *'It's OK to forgive my dad Sarah cos he needs us to forgive him, so does God, cos one day my dad might want to say sorry to God and we have to let God do all that, not us. And God knows what he did was bad and wrong.'*

I learnt a great deal that day from Anna Girl. This message came after several years of Anna being in her own process of forgiveness, but 10-year-old Anna's message just summed up the significance of what it means to forgive. It doesn't take away that what happened was 'bad and wrong', but it frees God to welcome back each and every one of us who run back to Him seeking forgiveness.

Chapter 8
Breaking Free

Sarah

In this chapter Anna describes how she came to the very difficult decision to break free from her parents. This was part of her journey; it is not a part of everyone's. However, there is a process of breaking free from the power of those who have abused. Some people find they are still behaving and responding to situations from the place of trauma, such as, 'this is how I had to behave then' or 'this is what I had to do then'. As healing starts some people become more aware of this and then find they are not allowing themselves to be free to respond in the way that they actually want to. Breaking free is about understanding what it is that is still tying the person into the memories, the repeated negative statements and the automatic responses that have been learned over long periods of time often as a way of surviving.

Noticing these patterns is key to understanding what it is the person is bound to. As they begin to notice their responses and then question them, there becomes a freedom that things can be done differently in the now. Writing, drawing and noting the body's response in situations all help to formulate an understanding of what is going on and therefore what can be done differently. It was from this process that Anna came to know that she wanted to be 'free' from her parents. In that process she decided she could not continue to have contact with them, but it was also about being free from the memories and the abusive patterns of relating with them. She came to realise that the relationships were causing continual trauma responses for her that she wanted to stop, for every part of her.

Anna

I'm not sure I can fully understand how God prepared my path for this to happen. Maybe I'll never know, but what I do know for certain is that the time became right, and when the time was right, suddenly, for the first time in my life, I did not feel afraid or bound to my parents in any way. For the first time in my life I had the strength, courage and wisdom to do what I felt was right for me. So much of abuse is about never believing you are brave enough or have the ability to do what feels right for you because that has all been lost in the act of abuse as well as in the place of fear afterwards.

When I think of the resurrection story, I always think about the image of the disciples at the empty tomb:

> *Simon Peter came, following him, and went into the tomb. He saw the linen wrappings lying there, and the cloth that had been on Jesus' head, not lying with the linen wrappings but rolled up in a place by itself.*
>
> *(John 20:6–7)*

When I look back at how I broke free it very much felt like those cloths wrapped around me in the abuse were unravelling.

I had tried to confront my parents several times about the abuse. I remember still to this day how terrifying it had been for me to firstly think about doing that and then trying to do it. I thought at the time I did it, I would lose my family for good. But I didn't. I felt that in order to still have a relationship with other family members, my sacrifice was maintaining a relationship with my parents. Over time, as I continued the relationship, the 'game' continued. Everyone seemed to carry on as if I'd never said what I'd said to my parents and it was as if we all fell back into a familiar pattern of denial. As I continued to maintain the relationship with my parents, it felt like they could just carry on as normal and leave the blame where they'd put it each time they abused me – into me.

That was until I began in therapy to speak about all the abuse for the first time. And then the real change of heart came as I journeyed deeper and deeper into my faith and relationship with God. Even though I had maintained a relationship with my parents as an adult, every time I saw them it had still been incredibly difficult. I hated seeing them even though I chose to do so. Somehow, I just swallowed the pain each time and got on with it, always hoping maybe the feelings would one day just go away and I could see them without all the pain. But things were becoming different with my faith. Sarah was helping me, all the little parts of me, to speak about the abuse. Sarah had listened to all the little parts of me. The little ones had, for the first time in their life, felt listened to and heard. They had, for the first time in their life, been loved, truly loved and comforted through all the memories and the pain. They had a voice with Sarah and knew that they weren't to blame. What my parents had done to us was abusive and should never have happened. All the little parts of me had been growing in their understanding of God and had been allowing Jesus with Sarah to start healing them and taking the pain away. The image of Baby Girl being cradled in the safe arms of Jesus for months and months was like allowing Baby Girl to start her life again in safety, true love and truth. I had asked for Baby Girl to be blessed again, to renew our baptismal vows, and Sarah did this with us one day. It was significant because it was about enabling the youngest part of me to grow up within me in the love and light of Jesus and not grow up in the darkness of abuse. Renewing our baptismal vows was symbolic. It felt like Baby Girl was given new life that day, as Sarah blessed her with oil.

As the adult, I was helping the little parts of me feel free to tell Sarah whatever they wanted to. At times it was as painful for me as the adult to hear their memories as it was for Sarah. When we weren't with Sarah, I let them write when they needed to, draw when they wanted to and be comforted through the pain. They loved being safe at home during these times, usually having a pyjama day, wrapped up in a blanket on the sofa watching children's films. But it gave the little parts of me a voice and comfort we had never had. I often used to think to myself, what would I be asking of someone else if they had taken on the care of children who suffered abuse? I would want that person to comfort them and help them learn how to feel safe again. Sarah did that for me, but I also had to learn to do that for myself.

Over time, the little parts of me had given their memories to God through writing letters to Him with Sarah and then burning the letters. And with all of this process, the ability to maintain a relationship with my parents was feeling more and more impossible. I occasionally met with my family, but being with my parents was suddenly becoming so difficult. I was taking all of me and the little ones absolutely hated it. Up until the time I had started integrating the little parts of me, I could be with my parents in a dissociated state, the way I had always survived. But now the little parts of me were present, fully present within me and with that I felt all the real emotion of being in contact with the people that hurt me. I felt within me, the 2-year-old part who was clinging on to me so tightly, it felt like her whole body was wrapped around me. I constantly had to reassure her that she wasn't going to be looked after by my parents because I looked after her now. 6-year-old was in tears within me most of the time, terrified she would be left there and not go home; she needed a lot of reassurance that we would be going back home. And Anna Girl found it incredibly difficult and NEVER wanted to see our parents ever again. She needed to email Sarah and hear back from her to help her through. I think Anna Girl was very angry with me for taking her, so it was very hard for her to let me comfort her.

But what I began to realise was that it wasn't just the little ones that didn't want to go, it was also me as the adult that didn't know if I could continue. It was perhaps part of the protective adult part of me that was feeling more and more maternal to myself. I found it hard to take parts of me in pain back into a very traumatic relationship. With my growing faith and developing understanding about truth, I could suddenly see my parents in a way I had never allowed myself before because previously I'd split off the parts of me that felt the pain of abuse. I suddenly saw my parents through the eyes of the terrified parts of me. So, it became impossible to continue the game of denial with my parents. And by 'game', I mean the abusive relational patterns. The 'let's pretend everything is normal' game. I now couldn't pretend it was all OK when I met with them. I sensed my father definitely knew something was different in me the first time I saw him after coming to faith. I felt he played on it (consciously or unconsciously). On one occasion he tried to intimidate me in front of others which was a familiar pattern of behaviour from him. But for the first time in my life when he did that, I looked at him and saw him for what he was and I walked away from the situation. I didn't play his game. I didn't stay 'frozen'. I took control and I took all of me away from the situation. It was an incredibly significant step in all the little parts of me beginning to trust that I had heard them, heard myself and I could keep all of me safe. I think I was beginning to realise that the relationship with my parents, in the way it was, couldn't sustain itself in the new life I was now building with God.

As time went on and my faith was growing, I was beginning to trust God more and more. I felt I was walking the narrower paths with God; they looked like the most unreal paths to take, but they were the ones I learnt to trust and follow. I remember feeling that wherever I was going in my life, I could no longer protect my parents. I was beginning to have a sense that in walking forward – wherever God was taking me – I needed to walk forward with all of me and all of my truth and I would no longer be able to keep the abuse hidden and separate. I felt it was becoming impossible to live my life whilst protecting my parents. Being in the place of denial now felt like I was living a lie and I knew I could no longer do that.

Sarah

I'm reminded in Anna's journey at this stage of the healing, of the journey of the wise men who sought and found Jesus. Their encounter with Jesus changed them. The poor and lowly king lying in a stable before them changed all that they would do going forward. The encounter meant that 'they left for their own country by another road' (Matthew 2:12). So, too, as Anna was encountering Jesus in her own life, her journeying was about walking a new path, taking a different route.

A person who is on their journey of healing and increasing faith changes. And within that change, their patterns of relating to other people also change. This is true for those who have been abused when I have encouraged the person to notice what is happening emotionally and internally. They begin to ask themselves questions such as 'what do I want to do about this?', rather than 'I must say yes' or 'I must respond in the way I usually do'. As Anna changed, others noticed the difference and the relationship changed, even though the other person may not have changed.

Relationships are the hardest thing we do as human beings. When our relationships are wrong, we need to ask ourselves the 'why' question and understand the part we are playing within it. When there has been trauma and abuse the reasons may relate to specific things remembered by the person.

One of the many people I worked with knew that she had a particular response to clergy who wore black shirts and black cassocks. Her response was to have an anxiety attack and then behave in a very odd way toward the person. If asked to do anything by the 'vicar' her response had always been that of a frightened child, not an adult's. Over time, having conversations and prayer she realised that she was treating every vicar wearing black as her abuser. She learnt in those situations to say to herself, 'this is not the abuser, I am safe now, I can leave the room now, I can leave the building.' It means the person who has been abused has to understand what is happening for him or her and then recognise why they are relating to someone in a particular way. The projection onto another person from relationships from the past can happen to all of us. Breaking free is about both understanding this and working on each relationship in the light of the 'new me'. In some situations, the relationships are abusive, and giving permission for the relationship to stop is part of the healing. The relationship cannot be maintained in a way that is healthy, often because the other person is unable to change.

Anna

Around the time all these changes were deepening within me, I saw a friend that I hadn't seen for many months. I spoke to her about the transformations that were taking place and how my faith had been helping me to feel freer for the first time in my life. This particular friend had never spoken to me about her own feelings about my relationship with my family but on this day she did. 'I never understood how you could carry on seeing your parents, letting them in your home and speaking to them,' she said to me. Everything that I had recently been mulling over in my mind came out in the conversation with her on that day. Suddenly as I spoke to her, I knew there was no way I could continue having a relationship with my parents.

The next morning, I woke up crying. I don't think I've ever woken up crying before! When I got out of bed, I prayed. I was still sobbing but the words that came out of my mouth were 'God I'm ready to be free of my parents; it's time now'. I couldn't believe how strongly I'd said that through all the tears – it came directly from my heart. I continued sobbing, saying 'I'm ready God, I'm ready God'. And I suddenly stood up but wasn't sure why I'd stood up because I hadn't finished praying. I was still crying. The crying got greater and greater as I talked to God about my parents and breaking away from them. It was something that I'd never before had the courage to do but now felt like the right thing to do for every part of me. I emailed Sarah and asked her to pray for me. I was still crying and miraculously Sarah called me back not long after I sent the email and offered for me to go and see her that morning. The work that I did with Sarah that day was probably one of the most significant on the journey.

Sarah

When Anna came to me and said she wanted to be free from her parents I realised this was a very big step. We talked about what that might look like and feel like as well as how she might do it. So, we prayed together and I asked her if she was happy to pray a specific prayer that symbolically cuts ties that had been formed between herself and her parents during the abuse (See Appendix 1).

Part of this prayer needs an understanding of the works of the devil or the forces of darkness. Paul suggests in his letter to the Ephesians that we need to be strong in the Lord and know that we wear the whole armour of God. Just as no one would run a marathon without preparing first, I would not have this time of specific prayer without some spiritual preparation. In order to prepare it is essential for both the person alongside as well as the person who is choosing to cut their ties or chains to read the Bible and to pray (Ephesians 6:10-18).

The prayer claims Jesus' presence and light to break the powers of darkness, which can form when there is abuse, rape, torture, murder, domestic violence etc. Essentially, it is a tie between the person and the event, and anyone associated with the event.

In Anna's situation the tie was with both parents who had been complicit in the abuse and whom she felt manipulated by. In the act of keeping things hidden they had left Anna with lots of very negative statements about herself such as 'It is all your fault' and 'You will never do anything worthwhile with your life'. It was the pretence that everything in their relationship was OK that became so hard for Anna, as it became an ever bigger lie.

Part of the prayer is about asking the life and light of Jesus to break whatever ties or chains or ways of relating have held the person for so long through the abuse. The prayer goes on to ask Jesus to stand between Anna and her parents. Jesus' crucifixion symbolises the breaking of chains between humankind and God. Therefore, He can be our only mediator so He is able to stand between Anna and her parents. On the cross, 'Jesus cried again with a loud voice and breathed his last. At that moment the curtain of the temple was torn in two, from top to bottom. The earth shook, and the rocks were split' (Matthew 27:50–51).

Jesus is now standing between them and he would mediate any future relationship. How would he do that? At that stage we did not know. But what we did know is that Anna's parents would firstly need to reconcile with Jesus before they could reconcile with Anna. What was important at this stage was for Anna to claim herself as the person God created her to be, away from the chain of abuse that she had been tied to. As Anna prayed the prayer with me and cried as she did so, she was owning the truth of the abuse and putting the choices and power back to those who did the abusing. Giving the power back to whom it belongs is a key part of breaking free.

I have found using this prayer about cutting ties or chains in relationships to be powerful for many people in my ministry.

Anna

There were two things that Sarah did with me that day which I found helpful: the cutting of ties, and understanding the passage in the Bible about the armour of God (Ephesians 6:10–18). It had taken a lot of courage that day to say aloud the prayer with Sarah about cutting ties. But I did it because it felt right for me and felt a helpful way to pray about all that was going on. It was powerful and the visual image of the cross and Jesus now standing in-between me and my parents helped me feel that they no longer had the same power over me. The younger parts of me were interested in the prayer and how it left us feeling. I knew that the cutting of ties between Anna Girl and our mother was not easy. Anna Girl had always felt like she had emotionally carried everything for our mother and it was very confusing and very complicated. She was angry about our mother but despite that she carried all her emotional 'baggage' and had always protected her emotionally.

The Bible passage about the armour of God also left me with another visual representation of how I could feel protected on a spiritual level. When I felt uneasy about all that I was doing at this stage of the journey, I prayed in the morning that I was spiritually putting on the armour. It was of great comfort to me, understanding that I could be protected.

Not long after this I had a week's holiday. It was a chance to rest and take in all the changes that were happening for us. I visited some amazing places which every part of me enjoyed. We were all able to have some fun which felt much needed. However, in amongst all that, something else was going on internally. Anna Girl really struggled with a lot of things during this holiday which I hadn't anticipated. Anna Girl was finding it harder and harder to have any communication with our parents. I remember the last day of the holiday we felt sick to the stomach at the thought of seeing our parents again. I realised that I was becoming less and less tolerant of them and knew more and more I could no longer live the pretence with them. I didn't feel I could face seeing them again or even speaking to them. The feeling of not wanting to see them was growing and growing inside me.

When I got back from holiday, I remember saying to Sarah, 'God is changing my heart'. I could literally feel my heart changing, my feelings towards my parents changing. The further I was walking this journey with God in His truth, the more I was being turned away from the lies and deception of my relationship with my parents. There was an upcoming family event that the little ones were beginning to fret about and we talked to Sarah about it. I think Sarah had said something to me like 'we really need to think about this for the little ones' and my response was 'I know they don't want to go; I don't want to go either'. I think Sarah was a little taken aback that for the first time me, as the adult, had said I didn't want to go. Sarah had always respected whatever I needed to do about seeing my family, even though it had been painful. But I sensed her delight in the courage and truth of my answer. It was true, my gut was firmly telling me 'you can't do this anymore'. I left Sarah's thinking, I have no idea how I'm going to do this, but I knew God would be alongside me.

Over the next few days, the sadness of it hit me. I had gone to a confirmation class at the cathedral. When we were at the cathedral, someone asked me, 'What have you given up for Lent?' With no warning, the tears just came streaming down my face and I had to leave; it was too personal to talk about. What I was giving up was everything; my relationships with my family. I had already given up so much and now this was going to be the greatest loss. I left in tears to go home to the comfort of my bed.

During conversations with Sarah we discussed the many ways that I could stop all contact with them, and we worked out a way that suited me. I truly felt that God had set me free from them. There was nothing that was binding me to them any longer. The linen cloths that had been wrapped around me in the abuse had now been removed. All of my old fears had somehow vanished. Even though it took great courage, I did break free from them in a way that felt right for all of me. It was the most difficult point on the journey.

As I broke free from my parents, I prayed for my mother and father and lifted them to God for His help. I prayed that they would be reconciled with God; it was the greatest gift I could offer to them. I couldn't reconcile my relationship with them, but God could, and I had to leave it at that.

Sarah

Breaking free is always hard, but over the years I have realised that the timing is always in God's hands. I need to let go, to be alongside and to trust in the work of the Holy Spirit, to free the person in the way that suits them and works for them. This takes a discerning heart and a close ongoing journey with that same Holy

Spirit myself. It is, as so much of this book says, about working with God and watching and waiting for the signs of the right time, then letting go and letting God be God. There is a breaking free in me as well because it is different each time.

As time went on from when Anna first felt she wanted to be free from her parents she found things began to change inside her that helped her discern the journey. Anna had been learning to listen well to the other parts of her and to give them space. She also began to realise how being with her family made her really feel and that she was not the same person any more as so much had changed in the healing journey. She found that if she was going to live in the light and the love of Christ, then being in relationships that were abusive felt, to her, like dying all over again, or being abused again. The time spent with her parents had become so painful for all of Anna.

Anna found ways to break free from her parents over time. As she did so, I prayed for her parents, just as Anna did. 'Lord please bless Anna's mother and father as they too face the truth. And Lord, as I try so hard to know, in spite of all of this they are still your loved children and you long for them to come to you. Help me with my anger and all the tears I too have cried as I have been alongside Anna. Help me to let go and let you take it out of my hands too. Give me wisdom and compassion in all the listening to and being with Anna. And please Lord, sort out anything else that is around that may still have a hold on her. Give me understanding and grace and show me how to proceed as I walk alongside this beautiful, brave child of God. Amen.'

Chapter 9
The Sadness that Comes with Freedom

Sarah

Breaking free and walking in her new-found freedom was immensely difficult and sad for Anna. She is not alone in that. Freedom means doing things differently and that means learning new ways of both doing things and being. I remember one of the people I was working with said to me, 'Sarah, I don't have any tools in the kit box for *this* me.' It is about learning from a new place, a different start. Each new part of the learning may bring with it a reminder of the past and the sadness of not being there anymore, however awful it was. It is a grief journey and will be travelled time and time again. Any relationship that breaks down is a grief journey and breaking free from the past and abusive relationships is no different. It requires courage and new ways of dealing with the overwhelming waves of sadness that can come. Anna talks about how she managed to walk through this.

Anna

Freedom has a lot of positive connotations associated with it because it is generally about coming from a place of darkness into light and I certainly wanted to be free in so many ways. But as I walked into freedom, very quickly I realised the reality of all the emotions that came with it – the first for me was sadness.

When God set the world free, he did this at a huge cost – his only son was crucified, in order for him to be resurrected and defeat death. Jesus experienced the darkness, the pain and the loneliness. Even Jesus did not feel close to God at that point of darkness, crying out to him, 'My God, my God, why have you forsaken me?' (Matthew 27:46). Jesus experienced the human pain of injustice, torment, abuse and persecution.

When the time was right to be free of the abusive relationship with my parents it wasn't a feeling of joy or relief that I felt; it was a deep, deep sadness, like grief. And this wasn't a grief or loss of a loving relationship, this was a grief and loss of the hope that one day my parents might love me. It was also a reality that they had not loved and cared for me as their daughter. This was a complicated relationship to let go of. As soon as I had broken free from them, the raw sadness hit me deep inside. The next morning the sadness grew. It was my own grief but also a knowing of my family's grief too. Nothing drew any comfort for me – I was reminded of that moment when Jesus experienced darkness on the cross and he no longer knew where his father was. The pain inside me was unbearable and I cried all morning.

What happened for Anna Girl that morning was also very difficult to go through. She had been so emotionally tuned to our mother and now had to let go of those ties. I couldn't stop the pain for her as she went through that, but I was there, with her. Just as Sarah had sat through pain with me, just as Jesus had sat through years of abuse with me, I held Anna Girl's hand that morning and hugged her through the tears as she went through the pain of breaking free. Anna Girl had always taken on pain from our mother and tried to protect her. She couldn't do it anymore and that was so hard for her, even though she knew we had done the right thing. I prayed with Anna Girl asking God to help her not to have to feel responsible and not to have to take on that pain anymore. I prayed for Jesus to take the pain from Anna Girl. Anna Girl was crying and crying as Jesus and I gently helped her know she could be free of this. It was such a sharp, raw pain.

The grief set in over the next few weeks and I comfortably sat in denial for a while keeping myself busy. But gradually moments of sadness crept in alongside other moments of freedom and joy. All the feelings sat hand in hand in the process and it was important to acknowledge that that could happen. 2-year-old Anna felt the loss quite intensely. I'm not sure whether it was because her understanding was so black and white, as it would be for any 2-year-old. But she often sat and cried in Sarah's arms saying, 'Me not got a mum and dad anymore'. Despite knowing she was safe, the pain of the loss wasn't any less. The sadness of the loss was a raw, aching pain.

As often happened, the pain would hit me when I was at the cathedral in the middle of a service. It was Pentecost and the sermon was preached by the Dean. What touched me during the sermon was when he spoke about the truth and living in the truth. He used an analogy of a brick or a block and that without the Holy Spirit things inside can feel unmalleable, as if it is impossible to mould or shape. But with the Holy Spirit things can slowly become malleable, begin to move and take a new shape. It was a real visual image for me about what had been happening inside us – things that I had never thought possible or would ever shift had begun to move and become possible. I had spent years in therapy trying to find a way to be free of the pain of abuse. And the therapy had only worked so far, and had almost chipped away at the brick a little. But with the workings of the Holy Spirit, the pain of abuse had changed shape. It hadn't removed the abuse from my memory, but it had slowly become formed differently within me. Yes, there was still some sadness and pain about it but it wasn't the same aching longing pains that I'd always had before. The pain was now moveable. I could feel it, understand it, pray about it and react to it within myself in a gentle, loving way. And that all changed the shape of the pain to a pain that was now malleable, not stuck.

The next day I sat with Sarah in her garden and she gently reminded me of the freedom I was walking into. To be in the freedom was amazing and I never underestimated that, but as I said to her it had come at a huge cost. It had changed everything in my life, nothing was the same as it had been, and I had let go of and lost an awful lot. The grief at this stage came over me in waves and it was really important to acknowledge the sadness that sat right within my freedom. I often felt like the place I was in at that time was an open barren plain. It was a desolate place, but it was open. I was in the light, not darkness. I was in the open and not in a dark enclosed tunnel like it had felt before. But it was an empty place at this stage on the journey. I often felt frustrated that I wasn't in a place surrounded by more people and things, but I had to accept the path I was on. I had to walk through the sadness and allow Jesus to walk alongside me with each step I took. I felt so fragile, so vulnerable and the feelings, emotions and memories that I had successfully buried for most of my life were suddenly just there within reach and all around me. I couldn't explain to anyone just how fragile I was at that point. Anything could evoke the pain and I could find myself sobbing out of the blue. It wasn't depression, it was pure, raw sadness that had now reached the surface. And there was actually nothing I could do at that point to make it better. I allowed myself to cry and tried my best to look after myself.

The little parts of me felt free to 'tell' Sarah about the memories of abuse in a way we never had before. I think it was part of the breaking free. Going through the memories at a deeper level was excruciating at times but again I had to let it be, let it come to the surface, be expressed and shared with Jesus and Sarah. Each time all of me went through memories Sarah held us and held us until the pain subsided. Sarah always said, 'you had no one to hug you then'. The sadness of her statement was true. Every time I had been hurt, I had been alone coping with the pain, both physical and emotional. This is where I learnt to dissociate in order to survive the pain. It was like I was dealing with the truth of the memories and all the pain that went with it, and that was unbearable. But the difference in the unbearable was that each part of me was now experiencing being comforted through the pain, knowing that they were loved and cared for. But also, by being comforted in this way each part of me knew I was alive and didn't have to shut down where it had almost felt like dying. Sarah prayed during these times and, through the love and prayers, each part was eventually able to feel calm – a feeling that we had never experienced whilst growing up. And when we were calm, I sensed the healing could start and we learnt to relax and be comforted.

There was something else that happened every now and then in those moments. When we were finally able to look at Sarah after the distress, there were times that we saw the distress and sadness in Sarah's eyes. No one had ever cried for us before, no one had cared enough to do that or show that. Sarah sometimes expressed her anger at what my parents had done and again it was an emotion no one had ever shown us. But it made each part of me feel really heard, believed in and completely loved. I'd never had a mother who showed disgust at what my father had done or sadness when I had been upset or scared or worried. I had only experienced a mother who sat mute while it happened and just told me not to be silly when I was sad or scared. I hadn't learnt that anyone could really understand me or my emotions or be that in tune with me. But seeing the pain in Sarah's eyes because of my pain was like connecting with another person in a way we never had before. This should have been a connection that I'd experienced as a child, but I realised the only connections I had made were full of trauma, stress and uncertainty.

But this time, when the little parts of me told Sarah the things they wanted to, I felt the distress of what they had said. At times I still felt a bit dissociated; I think the pain was still too much for me as the adult to bear. On one occasion, 6-year-old Anna asked Sarah to read back what she'd told her. For some reason the reading of it helped me to really hear it properly for 6-year-old. Later that day I also read something 2-year-old Anna had said to Sarah; I had also needed to hear that. I knew I couldn't function as split off parts anymore, but that meant even when it wasn't easy to hear, I needed to hear it. All the parts of me desperately wanted to be free of the trauma, but to be free meant that Sarah, Jesus and I had to walk through the horror of it. It was a necessary part of the journey into freedom and into the new, but it was with enormous pain and sadness. The more we let go, the more we realised how sad it was that our mother and father had never cared for us in the way we hoped and deserved. The sadness of what had not been was just as painful as the sadness of what had happened.

Sarah

Anna talks about the sadness of what had happened as well as the overwhelming reality and truth of what did not happen. She had not grown up in a 'normal, happy' family. The relationships were not about love, trust, mutual care and concern. I am constantly horrified by the ability of human beings to do dreadful and horrific things to each other. We see this daily in our news and can almost become immune to the impact of it as though we are trauma desensitised. It is important for anyone doing this kind of work not to become desensitised themselves to how bad it is. It is important not to lose some of our own humanity in the listening and being alongside.

Walking through the horror of it all, as Anna described, reminds me of a question I have been grappling with, theologically, for some time. How do we deal with evil? After much prayer and some research and more conversations with those who are theologically more knowledgeable than me, someone said one memorable day, 'Sarah, evil just is'. It is not something you can quantify or understand, it just 'is', I suppose in the same way, real goodness also just 'is'. It is not quantifiable. We feel it, we touch it and we recognise both, the 'good' and the 'bad'. For example, sometimes we hear people say about another person, 'goodness radiates out of her', and yet we cannot describe what we mean.

For me, being alongside Anna meant listening to the horror of abuse, and coming to terms with this, was my horror too. I am a human being and it was human beings that did this horror to other human beings. Sometimes after listening to people's abuse, I have sobbed in a way that has felt to me uncontrollable. What I have found helpful at these times is to take the dog for a long walk to reconnect with nature. It's as if there is something of the beauty of God in the expanse of a field and the delicacy of a buttercup. Sometimes I have gone and chopped some branches in the garden, as though in so doing I can remove or cut out the horror. Sometimes I have dug in the garden, getting my hand in the dirt of the soil and so finding newness and growth and hope. Even though listening to abuse is painful to hear, I know that Jesus is with me in the listening and I know that he can clear my head of most of the pictures that I'm left with. That process takes time and if I am honest, it also takes its toll on me. The exhaustion I can feel is part of that and I know that as I always said to Anna 'please look after yourself', we also had a deal that I would look after myself. I needed time and space to recover, in a different way to Anna, but yet in a crucial way for continuing to walk on with Anna. Finding appropriate strategies that work for me are important, so I can deal with the sadness and the loss and the pain.

It can be difficult to understand that Anna was remembering the abuse again after there had been so much remembering. But there was something different this time after she had broken free from family relationships. She was able to go deeper, so the healing was at a deeper level. In the first recalling of memories usually the part that is remembering is the only one who hears what is being said. As there is greater integration and more awareness of parts, the adult part is more able to hear what is being said. Sometimes the adult part is unable to listen as the younger part is speaking because it can be difficult to do the two things at the same time. Everyone is different; I have worked with people who are co-conscious all the time and others who have no idea what a part has said. In that situation, I always try to share what has been said with the adult part so that there becomes an acknowledgement and growing in understanding between the parts. Sometimes I summarise what has been spoken by younger parts, and as Anna shared, she was able to hear me reading what 6-year-old had written, so she too knew what had been remembered. I am aware that in some therapies and healing, a recording is taken so the adult part can listen later on to what has been said. I have chosen never to do this as, for me, it feels intrusive and can alter the process. I rely on the Holy Spirit to be the reminder and healer of what has happened because it enables the adult part to learn to listen to themselves. It is important for the adult part to hear and understand what has been remembered, not necessarily in full detail. The adult part then stands in the truth and that truth is all part of the journey of healing and freedom. The adult part is able to reassure and comfort the smaller parts knowing something of what has happened.

As people feel increasingly freer to share their experiences, it is important that I listen with an increasingly attentive ear, not just to what is said by the person, but to myself and the pain I experience as I listen. And then in the silence, to listen to God.

Listening to the pain is the hardest for many of us because it is the place of helplessness. It takes us into our own desert places. In Mark's Gospel when Jesus is tempted in the wilderness it says this: 'And the Spirit immediately drove him out into the wilderness. He was in the wilderness forty days, tempted by Satan; and he was with the wild beasts; and the angels waited on him.' (Mark 1:12–13). I found the following quote (from Michael Mitton's book *Wild Beasts and Angels*) helpful in explaining the place of both desert and healing:

> *'The more I reflect on the ministry of healing with all its joys, sorrows and mysteries, the more I am convinced that a spirituality of healing is located in the spirituality of the desert. It is in the desert that we are brought face to face with the wild beasts within and without, and we are made aware of the miraculous resources of heaven. The desert is the place of triumph and testing, of weary perseverance and unexpected revelation, of training in disciplines and discoveries of freedom.'*[8]

In my desert place I discovered that in this journey the wild beast is about owning my humanity. When I hear of the evil acts that humans have knowingly inflicted on another, I am then listening to the horror and torture and pain that ensued from it. It is also about bringing the real healing love of Jesus into the situation, that place of both triumph and testing. Holding the person in listening with Christ's love is borne out of an understanding of the desert place. It is as if in the darkest of places, the light is more apparent, the contrast is greater and the light shines brighter. That's when the transformation and healing happens. I gasp, standing in awe and wonder.

As I have been alongside Anna and many others in this place of loss and loneliness it has been about me holding out and holding on to the hope that is there with them in Christ. The light will shine again; the despair will turn to joy. The resurrection comes after the crucifixion. After surrendering himself to his death on the cross, Jesus embraced death to show the world that death does not have the last word on life. He also shared something of what it means to suffer and be in the place of helplessness and darkness in the tomb.

There is something very Christlike and profound about allowing the 'tomb times' when it feels as if nothing is happening and yet everything is changing. Joyce Rupp expresses something of this in her prayer:

O God,
I wait in the unending darkness
like a chrysalis on a lonely limb.

I am living in the dreadful 'in between'
of death and life, of darkness and light,
not coming, not going, just hanging on.

I fight the seeming emptiness
and struggle against required surrender.

Teach me to wait patiently,
while my wings grow strong,
for my time to fly has not yet come.[9]

This prayer is talking about that time when I can do nothing except to just be and to surrender. Jesus chose to surrender and in doing so suffered the crucifixion. As a consequence, he is able to bring freedom and healing to any situation we are in.

The loss for Anna as she faced the truth of what she had suffered was enormous. This was about her family, who did not behave as they could have done, the family whom she longed to be different. This is all about the desire of what might have been and the truth of the reality of how it actually was. The loss of family. The loss of her own relationships. The loss of childhood. The loss of innocence. The loss of self. When facing the loss, letting go of the grief has to be faced, and in that there is a place of surrender – a surrender to God. But in grief and loss there can be a despair that is overwhelming. How do we deal with that sense of being overwhelmed by it all? Part of the healing is about having someone alongside who can share with the feelings and be there; we all need such a person when we grieve. It is also about remembering that the despair and the feelings do not stay the same and, in time, slowly things change. Jesus did not stay in the tomb. As I stay alongside people, part of what I do is remind them of Jesus and his journey. I encourage people to think about how it can both inform and help them. A reminder that he did not stay in the tomb forever is crucial and that in his resurrection he appeared to the disciples bringing light, peace, hope and life.

And so, we wait in hope even within the darkest of our feelings. I sometimes ask people who are in this place of darkness, 'Do you believe that I am at the other end holding the light of Jesus?' If they do, I remind them to hold on to that belief. As time goes on, I ask again. Sometimes people will say, 'Yes I believe you are holding that light and actually I think I can see a small glimmer of light'. Later on, they may respond by saying, 'Sarah I can see more clearly. I think I am more than halfway through the darkness'. One of my favourite sayings that I was sent many years ago was, 'Sarah, keep punching the darkness until it bleeds light.' This is what those of us called to walk alongside are doing, by the grace and work of the Holy Spirit.

Anna

I would say it was there on that Pentecost Sunday listening to the sermon that I both realised the enormity of what I had done, and also had a sense of how different things were becoming for me. I began to feel that breaking free from my family had been right; each step I'd taken since then had given me confirmation of that. I knew that it was another part of the freedom and that to continue my journey it had been necessary. I'm not sure it's a necessary part of the process for everyone as it is such a personal decision within the healing.

One afternoon I found myself crying uncontrollably. The pain was the worst I had experienced in the journey. I knew I had to let it out, but I thought the tears were never going to stop. The memories were around, the loss was around, and the sadness poured out of me. 'Help me, Jesus!' I cried out. Parts of me wrote emails to Sarah through the pain and tears – I wanted them to not feel alone. Eventually I was able to breathe again, like coming up for air from wherever I'd been. Looking back, it had also felt like I was torn in the middle of the old and new. I was feeling the immense pain of the old combined with the unknown of the new. It was like having one foot in the loss and another attempting to step into the freedom, and both being seemingly overwhelming all at the same time. Jesus did provide comfort to me that afternoon. He didn't stop the pain, but I knew he was there and again that was what was different about having my faith in my recovery. I had the presence of Jesus who could tolerate pain at a level that no one could ever imagine.

I thought a lot about Pentecost during that time. I wondered about the disciples sitting in the upper room in Jerusalem (Acts 1:13). They had recently experienced the crucifixion of Jesus, probably terrified by all that had happened in his being sentenced to death and wondering whether they had misunderstood who they believed Jesus to be. They then encountered him in his resurrection and the shock that that must have been, but they had begun to enjoy his presence amongst them. And just as they perhaps became accustomed to that, they watched as he ascended to heaven (Acts 1:9). How on earth must that have felt to Jesus' disciples? I can't imagine. But what is apparent is, despite all that, they were obedient to his call and sat waiting in Jerusalem, awaiting the Holy Spirit as Jesus had told them. The disciples were in a new place of spiritual freedom, whether they understood that at the time or not. They were, just as I was during the time of Pentecost that year, wondering what on earth was about to happen. So much had happened for me, but I now felt a freedom I had never had. It was unknown territory, but I knew, as the disciples did, that I had to wait patiently, to be led forward on the new path I was taking.

Chapter 10
Holy Week and Easter

Sarah

It was strange this year finding myself in a new job. I realised I missed parish life and ministry especially during the busy formative major festivals, such as Christmas and Easter.

This year was different though as I knew that I would be taking advantage of being able to worship and be in Canterbury Cathedral and that the week would culminate in my being there for the first communion of Easter and Anna's confirmation. Her journey of healing and all that we had shared would make this a very special Easter. I was not disappointed!

The Archbishop of Canterbury was giving three lectures each evening of the first three days of Holy Week. Monday was on the risk of prayer. It was good and he spoke about the importance of prayer as being part of life and the way of building up our relationship with God. I sat there thinking about some of the people I see and how different the process is because we always pray at the end of a session and they know I pray for them. There is often an expectation from me that they will pray for me and most do. That is true with Anna – she knows that I pray for her and I know that she prays for me and that is an essential part of the relationship.

How do I pray for her? Sometimes I am very specific and pray that the pain she experiences will go, and that she will be able to give the situation she is remembering to God so she can forget it and be healed. Sometimes it is the request 'Please find her some work, please ensure money comes through, please keep her safe, please remind her of my love and yours Lord God.' At times the prayer is focused and at others it is a question of lifting Anna to the light and love of Jesus, so she knows it for herself. I sometimes imagine

God wrapping her round with a shawl of his deep, deep love and holding her safely; there was so little of that in her childhood.

The second evening of lectures, Anna was able to be there, so we sat together in the nave and listened to the Archbishop talking about the cost of reconciliation. What on earth does that mean for me and those I am called to journey with? It is a huge topic and I found what he said was not what I expected. I expected him to use as his text the passage where Peter, by a fireside, denies Jesus (John 18:25) and then the passage where Peter is restored back into right relationship with the resurrected Jesus. This was another fireside moment when Jesus asked Peter, 'Do you love me?' (John 21:16). I did not hear that much of what the Archbishop said because I was too busy thinking about what this meant for me. I am so keen that people are reconciled back to God and that any impaired relationship is restored. Sometimes there has never even been a relationship so actually finding one is all that really matters. I thought of Anna and her restored relationship with Jesus and all that she experiences when she worships in the cathedral; that surely is an amazing example of reconciliation. One of the key points to this is listening and I thought of the many hours that I have sat and listened to people and their precious stories – what a privilege.

The third evening, the Archbishop spoke about the celebration of witness and those times we are called to stand up for our faith and what that means. I have never been persecuted for my faith, but I still stand up for it. Then I thought of how healing is a celebration of witness. When God heals people and brings them into a new space and a new place there is a celebration of giving God the glory. WOW!

Maundy Thursday saw me in the cathedral again. In the morning I renewed my promises as a priest with the blessing of the oils which is so much a part of my present ministry. I knew that I was there for myself and all the work of healing in the diocese. I needed to renew my own vows to minister.

In the evening it was the washing of the feet and communion. I sat with Anna and saw it afresh through her eyes as she worshipped at a Maundy Thursday service for the first time. Jesus wants to wash my feet as a way of him being so much a part of my life – even in this intimate, personal cleansing moment. I reflected on how I am called to wash others' feet. There is something very intimate and trusting about washing peoples' feet. We no longer do this as a matter of course as was true in Jesus time; however, we are still called to that place of intimacy and care for others. This is expressed very differently in the 21st Century, but it needs expression, if we are to understand what Jesus said to his disciples, as he washed their feet (John 13: 1-20). That expression was what I watched and thought about. For me it is an encounter of listening well with our whole selves present, not doing other things at the same time, such as texting or eating. But it is about allowing silence to be part of the listening and being wholly present to the other person. It is both intimate and challenging. We see it perhaps most at those transition times, when we share in the birth of a baby by being there, or the death of a loved one, but also when we say by our very presence 'I am here with you; I have nothing to say but I am here'. At such moments we meet with the mystery of Jesus also there, kneeling, washing the feet of another.

It is impossible to wash another person's feet unless you actually kneel and there you are kneeling on the holy ground that is the other person's life and story. Wow! If Jesus does that for me, so am I called to do it for others. I knew that, for Anna, feet are not easy places of touch as there has been too much hurting of her feet in childhood. So how would Jesus touch her in this way and what, if anything, would make it alright? Would it be alright because it is Jesus? Or is it more to do with knowing the journey of healing so that it is the healed Anna who is being touched, and it is safe and alright in this new space when before it was so awful, so bad? Is it about speaking tenderly to Anna's feet so that they feel safe?

The service moves on to communion, the sharing of the Last Supper and from there into the watch as Jesus asks the disciples to stay with him in the Garden of Gethsemane and watch and pray – they fall asleep! As the service moves into this part, the cathedral is gradually placed into darkness with the lights going out one by one. It is extraordinary but quite frightening. Anna held my hand and we watched and waited together; not unlike the other times we have watched and waited and had a sense that Jesus is watching with us, waiting with us, holding faith and hope as we do.

Can I keep watch with Jesus in others' lives? Can I keep watch with Jesus in my own life? What would that look like? As I pondered this, I wondered if this was about keeping the space safe and keeping Anna grounded in both reality and in Christ. I realised that it is about that depth of prayer that is beyond words – as it says in Romans 8:26, the Spirit intercedes for us 'with sighs too deep for words.' That for me is what it is like. I am always reminded of churches where I have arranged the watch till midnight and as I have sat and prayed, I have remembered those who I have sat beside as they have died. This night was different; Anna was not dying, but as I thought about it I realised that part of her had had to die for her to be raised to new life. I was sitting beside her as some of her life died. It was given up to the glory of God so that the new could come. It cannot until the old has gone.

I am reminded of the verse 1 Peter 5:8–9 which is used in Night Prayer: 'Discipline yourselves; keep alert. Like a roaring lion your adversary the devil prowls around, looking for someone to devour. Resist him, steadfast in your faith'. I knew then that part of this for me is to keep praying that the light of Christ is able to shine so that the old can go and the new can come. What is the new like? The darkness of the tomb will lead to the stone being rolled away as Jesus bursting from the tomb comes in resurrection glory. Wow! So, we moved down into the crypt and sat there in the semi-dark praying and just being together. It was for me very moving and somehow what this Holy Week journey is about.

Good Friday I had advised Anna not to come to anything as I felt that she had already done so much letting go, so much being in the darkness, so much of the crucifixion story. I went to the cathedral again and was very moved by the service as I went forwards to honour and pause and kiss the cross. I thought of all that Jesus had been doing in my life; I thought of the times when he stands with me, for me, but more for the times when I listen to the incomprehensible evil that human beings are capable of with each other. I stood there and knew in a new way that Jesus had gone to the darkest, most evil places and brought light and life and change to them. He would have done that for any one of us and I wept as I realised the cost to him and my share in that.

Holy Saturday was a day of joy. I met Anna at the cathedral for the rehearsal of her confirmation with the Pastoral Canon, who allowed me to sit beside Anna for it all which reassured her, especially some of her frightened little parts. We then went out to lunch and chatted about the reality of being confirmed. WOW! What does this mean and how will it all work out? It is standing against her family who so often controlled her and did not allow her the freedom to follow her heart or to have a faith. This would be a new start in the whole process.

In the evening we met for the service. It started outside and we could not see very well but it was OK. Then the candles were lit as we brought the Light of Christ into the huge space of the nave and saw the light moving slowly through the building. It made me think that this is what Anna and I had done together, slowly bringing the light of Christ to all parts of her life and the difficulty and pain of the darkness; at times feeling as though it would have the last say. And then a glimmer of light, a breakthrough, a pinprick that gradually gets stronger and Christ the Light of the World shines through all the grot, all the mess and all the awfulness.

As Anna was confirmed and as we received the first communion of Easter, so that light became a triumphant alleluia. It was as if she too had burst from the tomb of darkness, of the evil of abuse, and had come into a place of acceptance and freedom. This was such an alleluia moment and one where, as I write and remember it, I want to cry and shout out loud all over again ALLELUIA! THANK YOU GOD!

Anna

It was a year ago since I sat in bed reading the Easter story in the Bible for the first time. It was a year ago since God's Word spoke to me so poignantly on Easter Day when I understood my Christian faith for the first time and when I declared my faith to God. Looking back, I realise this was one of the most significant Holy Weeks I will ever encounter, without any knowledge at the time that it was in fact Holy Week!

But a year ago I sat in my desert place during the week that was Holy Week; lost, afraid, lonely and battered by the abuse – battered by the pain of living as a survivor of abuse every day. I had given up and could do no more than lie in bed searching for a way to keep going, wondering if I could survive... again. But on that occasion, a year ago, I searched for God rather than something of this world to help me survive. And in searching for God, He gave me the gift of Jesus. Through God's Word, I met Jesus who offered Himself to me as He offered Himself to His disciples at the Last Supper, offered Himself to the Roman soldiers and priests who wanted to crucify Him and now offers Himself to every one of us. By His death on the cross He offers us a new life in him. Through the Easter story, I found hope in Jesus Christ.

A year on, my life had changed so dramatically! I sought healing from all that had held me in the pain of abuse. I had begun to let go of the abuse and started a long journey of forgiveness. I had integrated all the parts of myself within me. I'd shed so much of myself and what I'd previously held on to. But I'd found hope in Jesus who wanted me to just be the Anna God created me to be.

So, this Easter was significant in so many ways, and was a time to celebrate all Jesus had done for me since I found him in the

Easter story the year before. Is it any wonder that my confirmation coincided with this most poignant time of year for me? I guess not!

For many months all of the different parts of me had spoken to Sarah about being confirmed. Anna Girl was particularly interested in being confirmed. It symbolised something very special for Anna Girl about choosing to live a life in God and being free to make that choice, which we had not been able to in the past. Our parents had often been quite dismissive and negative about church. Anna Girl felt they had tried to prevent her having a faith because they made her doubt and didn't encourage her in her faith. Their acts of abuse towards us also left us doubting God.

Getting confirmed symbolised such a significant freedom in actively choosing to believe and live out our life in God. But it also symbolised a freedom from the abuse that had caused such doubt about our faith. It was about saying 'no' to all the lies and pain that the abuse had suffocated us in and saying 'yes' to the new life of hope Jesus offered.

But there was another significance about the whole event of being confirmed at Easter; and that was about being confirmed in Canterbury Cathedral, the place where so much of our healing had been happening. I often think of all the people over the centuries who have been on their own pilgrimage in that holy place; whether visiting, worshipping or ministering there. The physical space of the cathedral has been a place of pain, wonder and healing for so many and it was no different for me since I had been worshipping there.

The service of confirmation took place within the Easter Vigil service on Easter Eve. Every part of me was a mixture of anxiety and excitement. Sarah had helped us prepare and plan for our confirmation and we knew that she would be by our side throughout. That was crucial for all the parts of me. We had never had anyone by our side unconditionally as a child, through times of anxieties or on really special occasions. I had decided not to tell anyone about the confirmation other than one good friend who came along in support. I knew that all the parts of me just wanted to do this service without any fuss and doing it in that way just really helped us. The irony is being confirmed at an Easter Vigil service at Canterbury Cathedral doesn't lend itself well to not much fuss – ha! It's probably one of the most dramatic services in the year!

The service started outside at the great west door where a fire was lit, and the bishop lit the Easter candle. Inside, the nave was in darkness and we processed in with candles. The word nave comes from the Latin word meaning ship and the design of the ceiling in the nave represented the upturned bows of a ship. So, as we stepped through the great west door and into the nave, it represented something of the journey we had been sailing. The darkness during this first part of the service was hugely significant. It was actually very uncomfortable. Parts of me were very unsettled and restless. The readings in candlelight took us through the time of creation, the development of God's covenant with humankind to the coming of Jesus. But through this biblical journey, our own past was swarming around in our head. There were memories and feelings which seemed stuck in the darkness around us. Abuse as a child is dark. It's the most awful thing to experience that feels like an inner turmoil of being swept into a great storm at sea. Our whole world was literally tossed, turned and engulfed by the huge waves of abuse, time after time. As a child, my inner world had never known the calm of the sea, it was instead a constantly changing tide where we clung on to the side of the ship hoping to survive and not drown.

As we sat in the nave, we clung to Sarah, one arm wrapped around hers. We couldn't tell her what was going on for us as we sat there but she knew we were struggling at that point. As we sat and experienced something of the darkness of the abuse we had suffered and the darkness of having lived with it every day of our lives, the momentum of the service and the physical space of the cathedral eventually moved us.

Still in darkness with our candles lit, we processed through the nave and up the steps to the pulpitum which took us into the quire. Compared to the vast space of the nave, the entrance of the pulpitum which passes through to the quire is very narrow. It represented something so poignant about our faith and that moment a year ago when we found our faith: 'Enter through the narrow gate; for the gate is wide and the road is easy that leads to destruction, and there are many who take it. For the gate is narrow and the road is hard that leads to life, and there are few who find it' (Matthew, 7:13–14).

As we came from the dark, vast space of the nave, which had represented something of the destruction of having lived a childhood of abuse, we followed the light of the Easter candle into the quire.

As we got into the quire and stood near to the high altar, the lights came on and the bells were rung. We were welcomed into God's resurrection glory with light, music, bells and the singing of 'Alleluia, Alleluia'. Our journey had led us to understanding something of God's kingdom and, most beautifully, the high altar is surrounded either side with statues of angels. These angels look on, watch and pray, and represent our healing and heavenly protection. During every Eucharist when 'Holy, Holy' is sung we have stood studying these angels and all that they mean to us. And tonight, it felt as if the angels were rejoicing with us.

Our confirmation was the next part of the service. It symbolically came at the physical point of the service of having made the choice to follow the journey into the light and truth of God's kingdom. So, with that we walked up the first few steps of the high altar. The Bishop of Dover was seated, and we knelt down in front of him. 'Anna,' he said, 'God has called you by name and made you his own.' Those words meant everything to us: all that we had journeyed with God in being healed from abuse. Being called by our name and made God's own is the journey of being the Anna God created, not the Anna that had been abused. And with that the bishop confirmed and anointed us. It was such a significant moment in feeling named by God.

Later in the service, as I knelt down to take the sacrament, the words seemed to come from nowhere but were so powerful: 'Our dad can never hurt us again' we said in our head, 'our dad has no power over us anymore' we said next. The power of abuse was being washed away from us at the altar.

The physical space held us in the newness of our true life in Jesus. From the darkness, we had come into the light of love, truth and freedom. After receiving communion, we were given an Easter candle that represented all of that. Holding that light, we experienced the mystery of God's love and healing.

I wasn't prepared for the next emotion which came from absolutely nowhere. Anna Girl said to Sarah; 'I think the Holy Spirit has given us the gift of Joy'! It was a feeling like no other that I'd experienced; it was just pure joy. After so much pain and being in darkness for most of our life, the Holy Spirit cloaked us in joy just as the angels surrounding the altar had rejoiced with us. When the service ended, we walked arm in arm with Sarah back down the quire following the bishop, but inside we skipped! We were dancing with joy.

Epilogue

Sarah

As Christians we are all pilgrims on a journey of life and the journey requires us to be honest and authentic in the travelling. For survivors of abuse there is a need to relearn patterns of being and ways of living as they walk in the newness of their healing. So much of the past has been about how to survive and some of the strategies to survive have been focused on ignoring emotional feelings as well as feeling stuck in negative thought patterns such as 'I'm a failure'. As people receive healing and find they are relearning how to live anew in Christ, it is so important to encourage the person to be gentle with themselves. The truth is, healing is exhausting and learning not to fight the exhaustion is key to doing things differently. It is about allowing yourself to walk very slowly in the new instead of trying to run ahead. It is not easy: some days it is very hard, some days it can be painful, some days it is full of temptations, but some days the sun shines and all feels well. It is never static. The need to be patient and wait for the new becomes a daily way of life rather than just a one-off experience. I often describe this as a daily dying and rising to new life. We all do the Easter story, often in just a day; that dying and rising. Hanging onto the hope of new life helps us to cope with the darkest of times. As the psalmist sings, 'weeping may linger for the night, but joy comes with the morning' (Psalm 30:5). Walking in the new is about a renewed sense of deeply knowing that joy will come. We need to focus on remembering the moments of real joy, of Gods miraculous intervention, of the healing that we know and rejoice in.

As I minister healing to those who have suffered, it is about holding out the hope of the joy that will come – the alleluia moment. I give thanks to all those who have blessed me as we journeyed together. I hope this book encourages all of us in our own healing journey as we offer companionship to others on the way. As in the story of the disciples on the Emmaus road, (found in Luke 24:13-35), may we too know the surprise and joy of Christ's resurrected presence, bringing healing and peace.

Anna

As time went on I felt like I'd walked into a new land. It reminded me of stories I'd read in the Bible, mainly the Old Testament when God asked people to move into a new land and that somehow felt symbolic of the journey I was on. In this new land I suddenly felt as if the abuse had been lifted from me. It was surreal after carrying it for so long and being swarmed by it to suddenly feel like I could move around without it being all around me. But it felt calm and free. I actually felt free. I had experienced glimmers of freedom at times but I began to feel really free. In these early days I continually thanked God for bringing me into this space. When it had seemed impossible on the way I kept trusting in God and now I sensed that He had actually set me free. 'The truth will set you free' was where my spiritual journey had started and it became a reality for me. I could be free; I am free!

For the first time in my life I felt that there was nothing more for me to do and by that I mean there was no more processing, letting go, battling, 'work' to do about the abuse; it was gone. It wasn't gone completely as it would remain part of me and my life, but it was gone from dominating every breath and every step I took. I had had no idea that was ever possible but it happened; it really can happen.

So what was this new space like? It felt safe for the first time in my life and that's a hard concept to describe. But it felt like the abuse and my abusers were so far away from me now and that I could now walk around free. I no longer needed to be afraid. I had let go in every way possible. It was a light place to walk, not just light in a light/darkness sense but it physically felt lighter too. This is perhaps the feeling that I had hoped for as a child but never knew existed. So I chose to do nice things as I began walking in the new space. Every part of me was excited, happy, content and free for the first time.

There will always be times that the past affects me and times when I feel sad or angry. But the difference now is that I'm not stuck in the trauma. So if I do have memories or painful feelings, I can now go through that from a new place, not from the place of the terrified parts of me.

As I walked on, I knew that my past would always be my past, part of who I am. But it had slowly, over time, become less and less of my identity. As I learnt more and more about every part of me and grew in my relationship with God, I began to have a greater sense of my identity as the Anna that God created. It was what I had set out to find. Even though it had been difficult to see at times, God enabled my eyes to see and my ears to hear the Anna that God created. Thank you, God!

Appendix 1
Services and Prayers as a Resource

These are unpolished and incomplete draft services with ideas and suggestions. They are written so that whoever uses them can adapt them for individuals or groups in any setting.

I would always recommend full co-operation and involvement with survivors, before using any of these services or prayers.

A sample Christian service for survivors of abuse

If this service is used for survivors of abuse by clergy or a Christian Institution, please be very careful about the venue as some people will find any Christian symbols will act as a trigger for memories of abuse. Any environment that feels 'unsafe' will disable those who may want to come. I have found a cafe-style type environment, an informal setting, to be very effective, with prayerful, caring and loving people around enabling those who come to feel safe and 'allowed' to do what will help them.

Our journey of healing requires immense courage
and takes us from......
darkness to light
from despair to hope
from being chained to being free.

Today we pray that all of us may take some steps on
Our own journey of healing.

Welcome/introductions

We are meeting in the presence of God
Who knows our needs
Hears our pain
And heals our wounds.

In Jesus Christ, we hear the Good News
That God is like a mother hen
Who shelters her chickens under her warm wings.
We believe that God is love
In Jesus, we see a God
Who wept for the people of the world
And weeps with our wounding

In Jesus, we see a God
Who reaches out with healing hands
Who sees our pain and makes us whole.

Psalm 107:13–14. And 116:1–2

They cried to God in their trouble,
And God saved them from their distress;
God brought them out of darkness and gloom,
And broke their bonds asunder.

I love God, because God has heard
My voice and my supplications
Because God has inclined his ear to me
Therefore I will call on God as long as I live.

2/3 worship songs

Prayers of forgiveness following an introduction are based on Daniel's prayer of representational confession (Daniel 9). These prayers are specifically for the church setting but could be adapted for any institution or situation.

O God, who reconciled the world through the
death and resurrection of your Son Jesus,
help us today to believe in that forgiveness and reconciliation.

Lord I cry out to you for the church. Your Word
says we can cry to you O God to forgive and heal us.

Silence... *Lord forgive us and heal us.*
As a member of the church I ask your forgiveness
for all the times the church and its members did not
listen to the truth of the abuse suffered.

Silence... *Lord forgive us and heal us.*

Jesus, by your death and in your resurrection
I ask your forgiveness for all the times church
authorities and individuals misused their power
and abused those in their care.

Silence... *Lord forgive us and heal us.*

Lord God I cry out to you.
Please forgive me as I stand here in this place: for all the evil
acts of inhumanity and abuse person to person that have
happened.
I pray that we may do all we can to ensure
safe and loving places where we can all grow and flourish.

Silence.... *Lord Jesus come and heal us.*
Come and free us.

In the name of God the Creator
In the name of Jesus the Son,
In the name of the Holy Spirit.
Amen.

Hymn/song
Poem/other reading
Hymn/song

Reading: Mark 5:24–34 (Or another suitable for address)

Address/sermon not more than 10 mins. (Generally, people in these circumstances cannot concentrate)
Time to move around the space, to light a candle, do something creative such as make a bookmark from scratch art card, write a name or memory and watch it burn in a container outside, write new one liners, have a tea/coffee, chat to someone, go to one of the prayer stations to be prayed for, be anointed... whatever seems right to set up in the space you have.

The words of hope on the service sheet will be spoken aloud; music may be played quietly.

Words of hope

You are precious in my sight and honoured and I love you. Isaiah 43:4.

I am a new creation, no more in condemnation. Romans 8:1.

And you will know the truth, and the truth will make you free.John 8:32.

The Lord is my constant companion. Psalm 23:1

On the day I called, you answered me. Psalm 138:3.

He will take delight in you with gladness. With his love He will calm your fears. Zephaniah 3:17

God is our refuge and strength – an ever present help in trouble. Psalm 46:1

All say the Lord's Prayer together
Closing song/hymn

Blessing
Invitation to have prayer ministry, refreshments, conversation **and** leave.

Prayer – Breaking a Soul Tie

There are generally three stages of prayer in the breaking of a 'soul tie'.

1. A prayer that expresses an understanding of repentance for any contribution to the problem as well as a seeking of forgiveness of the other person/people.
2. The prayerful breaking of the tie in the name of Jesus.
3. A prayer for the breath of the Holy Spirit to bring healing and restoration with a final prayer and sometimes anointing with oil to seal the time of prayer.

An example of a prayer follows but I cannot stress enough it is really important for each person to write and own their own prayer. This is just a guideline.

Gracious God I come to you in the name of Jesus and in the power of the Holy Spirit and acknowledge an unhealthy tie between me and.......N....... I choose to forgive ....N...... and give him/her/them to you for your forgiveness especially in all the ways he/she/they hurt me. (If at all possible name any specific hurts and actions.)

If there is any way that my forgiveness is incomplete, Lord, I ask you Jesus to enter into it and complete it for me. I also ask for your grace to live in the stream of this forgiveness more each day.

I ask your forgiveness for any ways or actions that have been part of the problem rather than part of the solution, and for all the ways I have hurt.......N.... (This part may not be necessary but in the case of adult broken relationships, such as a divorce, it may.)

I now ask for the grace to forgive myself and help me to leave this all behind me.

Believing that I come before you Lord as forgiven, I ask you in the name of Jesus, by the power of the Holy Spirit to cut every unhealthy tie that exists between me and ....N.......... I ask that you would place the cross of Jesus firmly and completely between me and ....N...... so that from now on any relationship we may have is filtered by your cross.

I now in Jesus' name give back to.....N..... any part of him/her/them that stuck to me no matter how that happened. I ask that by the power of your Holy Spirit, you would heal and restore ....N....

And I release.....N... into your perfect plan for his/her life.

I reclaim my identity in Jesus Christ and I ask for a fresh outpouring of your Holy Spirit to fill me and minister to me restoring me to God. (If appropriate you may pray a prayer of blessing on the person if that feels possible and he/she is still alive. This is more relevant if the relationship is ongoing.

Finally I seal this prayer in the name of Jesus Christ. I seal it so the healing cannot be lost or stolen or destroyed. I seal it against doubt and any attack of the enemy. I seal it in the name of the Father, the Son and the Holy Spirit to whom be all the praise and honour and glory. (Anointing may take place at this point with oil on the forehead.) Thank you, Jesus, Amen.

Prayers

I have used the following at different times with people or they have adapted them for themselves.

God of freedom and liberation,
You have brought me out of the bondage of abuse.
I now release my abusers to you,
Recognising that they have no more power over my life.
I celebrate the gift of free will that was your blessing to me
And on all your people from the dawn of time.
I invite the creative power of your love,
That you may work through me

To bring your healing to others who have suffered abuse.
I ask for the wisdom to use my own experience
To increase other's awareness of violence and abuse.
Here I am Lord. Show me the 'how' for your kingdom and your glory.
Amen.

God of creation, I believe that you created me in your own image
And that your nurturing presence is with me.
I believe that you desire healing and wholeness for me,
And I rededicate myself today to the journey of healing I have begun.
I pray that you will be with me and give me strength
To overcome the effects of abuse in my life.
In Jesus' name. Amen.

God of compassion and healing, who desires the wholeness of all creation,
Look with mercy on those of us who struggle to bring together the pieces of
Our scattered, even broken, lives.
Comfort us in the pain of facing the truth,
Heal us in all the places we have been hurt
And bind us together in the strength of your love.
In Jesus' name we pray. Amen.

God our Father
In loving care your hand has created us,
And as the potter fashions the clay,
So you have formed us in your own image.
In Jesus Christ you have shown us
Love in action and the promise of eternal life.
In all our hellos and goodbyes

May we have a sense of your presence
Waiting to welcome us to the eternal hello in heaven.
In Christ's name we pray. Amen.

We are God's holy people in God's holy space.
Help us to remove from our hearts all that has caused us pain;
Help us to right the wrongs, however small,
That we have caused others.
Help us to put aside the trivia and niggles of life's journey
And rest in all that is good and all that is yours.
Help us to reach out to our enemies,
To the unloved, the socially outcast and the marginalised,
So that all we behold can see in us
God's forgiving eyes, Jesus' healing hands
And the Holy Spirit's light and comfort. Amen.

This is a prayer I wrote for a group of people who had experienced a traumatic event:

O God whose longing is to reconcile the whole universe inside your love,
Pour out your abundant mercy on us here today;
For we are fragmented and torn apart by recent events where we live.

Lord hear us
Lord graciously hear us.

For our failures to protect each other,
To try and understand each other,
And our failure to listen well to each other.

Lord Jesus forgive us and heal us.

For our failures to resist the bitterness and gossip
Which poisons and sours the gospel message of love and peace.

Lord Jesus forgive us and heal us.

For our failure to present a wounded world with hope;
For our failure to show peace and harmony
In a true and loving community of men and women.

Lord Jesus forgive us and heal us.

May the God of love and peace forgive us and heal us
By the death and resurrection of Jesus Christ. Amen.

Blessing

May the God of all ages, who is ever young,
Bless, inspire, and warm you.

May the risen Christ, a Living mystery among us,
Burst the tombs which deaden you.

May the Holy Spirit, who is the dance of life,
Be your constant companion and guide.

The blessing of God – Father Son and Holy Spirit –be with you
And all those you love and pray for this day and always. Amen.

Appendix 2
Healing Stories at Significant Times in the Year

Anna Girl and the bonfire

Anna

It has often been the simplest of things that have been so profound and I guess that is part of what Jesus tried to explain in many of the parables he told.

Anna Girl and Sarah had had an agreement for many months about a bonfire! After many trips with Sarah to the bonfire to burn letters to give to God she had always asked Sarah when she would have a proper bonfire. Sarah had agreed that when she had a bonfire, she would invite Anna Girl over. One Sunday afternoon, out of the blue, Sarah emailed Anna Girl to do just that and together that evening Anna Girl and Sarah had a bonfire. It sounds simple and ordinary but for Anna Girl it was far from that. Firstly, Sarah had remembered her, but not only remembered her, she had remembered the promise they had made. Secondly, Anna Girl was so happy to be invited to go and do something with Sarah, just out of the blue. For Anna Girl that meant that Sarah wanted to spend time with her and that was so important to Anna Girl who had felt no one had wanted her.

And then there was something so magical for Anna Girl about building a bonfire with Sarah. I realised afterwards how important trust had been and the thing that struck me most was that in order for a child to 'play' with an adult there needed to be trust. Anna Girl was not afraid to 'play' that evening; building the bonfire had been like playing for Anna Girl as she found things to put on and decided where to throw things in the bonfire. It felt like she was playing, but I knew she only felt safe enough to do this because she trusted Sarah. Anna Girl was relaxed, happy and content in a way she never had been before.

We all felt the joy of Anna Girl and that was the other most wonderful thing. It wasn't about Anna Girl in isolation; we all enjoyed her having fun and being the 10-year-old she had been afraid to be. She went home sooooo happy that evening telling Sarah it had been the 'best evening ever'. Inside me, she was constantly chattering away with joy for a good while after that and into the next day.

Sarah

It was a beautiful day and the weather was due to get bad. We had a mound of stuff to burn and I thought, 'what I need this evening is to have a bonfire; it will help me let go of a difficult day'. I remembered that Anna Girl wanted to be there so out of the blue I invited her. The answer was an immediate YES so I set it up and did other things. Anna Girl was surprised that I had not lit the fire before she arrived and I think as I explained why, very pleased. She watched me light it and we waited and watched the flames and the direction of the smoke. We discussed it all and what to put on next. At times we had to wait and Anna Girl said she didn't like waiting. I teased her and said I know but then as we were chatting the flames came through and so we put more on. It was great and such fun. We walked round the garden a bit and it gradually got darker so we could see more of the fire. When we had really burnt everything we went in for a hot chocolate and just chatted; before leaving we checked the fire was OK and all was safe. It was such a simple, lovely time with fun and laughter. As she left we laughed and I think we all felt better. The spontaneous part of the invitation was very important. It was a deeply God moment just because it was so normal and such fun. Thank you for coming and sharing it with me tonight!

Anna Girl

For a very long time I kept asking Sarah 'When are you having a bonfire?' She said she would tell me when she did and I could go and help her. I liked bonfires but I didn't know if it would really happen, or that Sarah would remember and want me to help her. I know Sarah loves me but I still get worried sometimes she might forget me, even though Sarah always says 'How could I forget you Anna Girl?!'

We were at the beach and Anna looked at her emails and there was one for me from Sarah saying she was thinking of having a bonfire. I was so excited. Anna texted Sarah back and said I was very excited and would love to go. I kept thinking 'I can't believe Sarah remembered'. She remembered me and our promise about the bonfire and she also wanted me to go – wow! I never really think anyone wants to spend time with me. I'm trying hard with Jesus to stop thinking that but it is taking lots and lots of practice.

We went to Sarah's and I couldn't see the smoke when we drove past. Sarah came to find me from the car and I gave her a really big happy hug. Sarah said she waited for me before she lit the bonfire because she thought I'd like to see that. I was so happy. I watched Sarah light the bonfire and start to put things on that would burn easily. She asked if I wanted to put something on but I wasn't sure and I said 'I'm just going to watch'. Sometimes I do that when it's something new because I get a bit unsure, so I just watch instead. I get a bit worried I might do something wrong. But then Sarah gave me a big branch and I put it on the bonfire. I liked helping and it was OK cos Sarah doesn't mind what I do, even if something goes wrong. I found big branches that I wanted to put on, then I asked Sarah if I could put a pine branch on. 'It might go crackly,' she said. Crackly would be fun, so I threw it on the top and it went really crackly and made really big flames!! The flames were so big so Sarah put some damp leaves on to quieten it down, but then all the flames went! Sarah said the flames would come back but I'm not very patient so she took me for a walk around the garden. When we went back, just as we walked to the bonfire, all the flames started again – hurray! So me and Sarah made a really big bonfire with all the other things to put on it. I liked finding big logs to throw on. It was lots of fun. I love doing fun things with Sarah cos I feel safe with Sarah and that means I feel safe to have fun and I don't have to worry about anything.

When we finished making the bonfire, we went inside and Teenage Anna made me a really nice hot chocolate, cos she makes the best hot chocolate! Me and Sarah sat and looked out of the window at the bonfire and I talked to Sarah. We went to check on the bonfire before we went home and it was all burning down. I was so happy when we drove home and went to bed and even when we woke up the next day! Thank you Sarah and God for my special bonfire night – it was the best night ever xxxx

Christmas 1

Anna

This Christmas I made a brave decision, a decision that seemed in contrast to the human expectations of celebrating the day with close friends or family. I knew in my heart that I needed to spend it alone. This was the first Christmas with all parts of me integrated and my first Christmas since stopping all contact with my parents. Joining in anyone else's celebrations just did not feel right or true for me.

I needed to be true to me, and me within Jesus. The truth hit me painfully on Christmas Eve. I was standing in the kitchen making a drink and, as I was stirring the drink, I thought about one member of my family who I knew could not bear my suffering. I could see her reaction to my suffering so clearly in my head. She was needing to avoid it at all costs and it made me think about why she doesn't contact me or respond to my truth – because she can't go near the pain. And then I saw in my head my family all continuing a family Christmas 'as normal'. It hit me hard that other family members continued to choose my abusive parents over me who had suffered. On one level I knew they chose that for their own protection and self-preservation. But another part of me just could not comprehend it. It is not for me to judge their choices as I continually give that to God – He is the judge of that. But I do have to live with their choices and that is painful.

I went and prayed after being hit with all this and I sobbed with God. It wasn't a 'this is not fair' pain; this was a pain of living in the truth. Sometimes people do not always see the full reality of abuse. The acts of abuse itself were awful but so were the ongoing consequences. I lived my whole life being controlled by my family, passively controlled, to keep quiet and pretend everything was OK. Every Christmas I had to 'perform' and by that I mean that I had to pretend that I was happy, that I was part of a happy family, having a happy time celebrating Christmas. It had been my job, in particular, to be fun and cheerful and ensure everyone else was happy too. My job in the family at Christmas had been important for years and years. And for years and years I had performed this role beautifully. I turned up, brought Christmas cheer, kept everyone happy, provided laughter and fun and that kept everything well – for them.

But this came at huge cost to me. What no one saw was that before Christmas I was usually ill, didn't sleep, was fearful, afraid, anxious and did not want to go. On my journey home I was upset, flat, exhausted and felt like I'd lost myself. The pattern of abuse continued. They weren't performing acts of abuse, but they were continuing the cycle of controlling and silencing me.

I was not living in the truth. I was so far from it I didn't even know what truth was. And that's one part of the impact of abuse; it's like constantly being engulfed in a dark mist that makes you confused and doubt your own truth let alone being able to see or know what your truth in God is. But this Christmas had come after beginning my journey of truth in God. A year ago I still hadn't been strong enough in that truth to say 'no' to my family, but this year I had!

This Christmas Eve, for the first time in my life I sit here with no impending anxiety or fear of needing to see my family and be silently abused in that. I did not need to go and be the person everyone needed me to be. This Christmas Eve, I sit here knowing the full truth but not just knowing it – I'm living it and staying in it. The truth I know is that I am loved by God who gives me all the strength I need. The truth is I feel free. I feel at peace, I feel lonely, I feel sad – I feel a mixture of things that are true to my Christmas this year. But I stayed true to my decision to be alone, to keep every part of me safe and to put my faith and trust in God with that decision. He has not let me down, but is holding my hand and guiding me through the brave steps I take. This Christmas I can be the person I am, not the person an abusive family needed me to be; to stop me from telling them how badly they had treated me. I served a great purpose to my family in performing my duties of happiness well; I kept them away from truth. This year, I stand in the truth not only for myself in God, but I stand in truth for my family.

The reality of Christmas is that Mary and Joseph, who obeyed God's will for them, found themselves alone despite being in Joseph's home town. Nobody welcomed them in and supported them, probably for fear of the truth of Mary's pregnancy, because the couple were not married. It was perhaps easier for people to dismiss them rather than understand their situation. Jesus was born to his parents in a stable. It looks picturesque now we understand the significance, but at the time a stable was a pretty bleak and isolating place to be. But Mary and Joseph had obeyed God. Those that came to see him had also believed in the messages and signs God had sent about the truth of who Jesus was.

There are choices we all make. God's will for us isn't always straightforward or 'normal' and listening to his truth takes time and can take us out of our comfort zones. I know my family need to stay in their comfort of pretending. But now I live a life with God I can only live my life in truth and this Christmas that's what I will be celebrating. It's not pain free, but it's truth.

Christmas 2

Anna

I have been feeling sad for a few days. It's Christmas Eve and as I chose to spend another Christmas alone there is much on my mind. It's as though this time of year magnifies pain within me. Just as God brought His promised Son into the world as a vulnerable infant, there is something about this time of year that brings my vulnerability to the forefront. Mary and Joseph were also vulnerable – a young unmarried couple bearing a child with nowhere to stay. And Jesus, a tiny human being, born in a stable.

I'm always reminded at this time of year of the choices I have made as well as the choices my family have made. All our choices lead me to being isolated from my own family. The consequences of parents who chose to harm me and continued to pretend nothing was wrong. Family members who choose to maintain the 'status quo' with my parents. My choice to stand in the truth with Jesus, which means I no longer sit in a place of pretence with my family. It's sad. There is sadness in all that's happened – my family and my identity in my family torn apart by abuse. The sadness of humanity that has been since time began.

But by not pretending, by being alone at this time, I can lay myself open before God: my true bare self, my weaknesses, my fragility, my sadness. As God fulfils His promise to mankind through the gift of Jesus, I can look at the fragility of how He brought Jesus into our midst. The vulnerable people that God chose to help Him fulfil his promise – vulnerable yet righteous, faithful and obedient. They too had to lay themselves open to God, to put aside all expectations, fears, worries, sadness and remain true to what God asked of them.

In the quietness of Christmas Eve, I weep with God with the pain I feel inside me. But yet, I rejoice with thanksgiving that he has brought us salvation where one day I shall suffer no more. Mary endured the pain of childbirth, felt adoration at the birth of the Son of God, and shared his birth with strangers, but learnt through those strangers that Jesus was holy indeed. Pain, joy, grief, thanksgiving and the unknown were likely to have been the feelings Mary experienced, not only from the time of visitation by Gabriel, but throughout Jesus' life and her own life.

****

How hard is it for us to sit with the Nativity? It's a week after Christmas now and it's something that I've been thinking about all week. This verse has been in my mind:

'But Mary treasured all these words and pondered them in her heart' (Luke 2:19).

She had just been visited by the shepherds who had told her all that had been told to them by the angels. Christmas can come and go in the world so quickly and by Boxing Day the consumerism of our society tries to move us on to new and exciting things. But what is happening in the Nativity is the most significant thing that has happened to mankind. The fulfilment of God's salvation is lying in a manger.

So, what happens if we dare to sit with Mary at the time of Jesus' birth? What happens if we choose to sit with Mary and look at the Christ Child in front of her? What happens when we just sit and ponder all God's Word in our hearts, like Mary did, and see His fulfilment of salvation in the flesh, lying before us?

It is miraculous and undoubtedly life-changing to sit with Mary in the Nativity. In front of us, we see God's pure love brought before us, to be among us. The Christ Child is helpless and vulnerable as we all are. But the Christ Child, in all His vulnerability will fulfil God's promises to us. To rush away from the Nativity is to turn away from Christ, to turn away from God as the first creation did in the Garden of Eden. Christ lies before us, for us to turn to and to sit with; with a knowing that he loves us for all eternity. To sit with Mary in the Nativity is to sit with God in the Garden of Eden, faced before Him, knowing that we are His beloved children who will bring us into His kingdom to come.

Thank you God, Amen x

The Road to Damascus and the Empty Tomb

Anna

The few times that I have now found myself in a new land with God, the more I have begun to ponder the process. The Old Testament details many accounts of God having moved his people to a new land. In fact, in the New Testament, God asked Jesus to enter new lands or towns since the time of his conception and in his early life. The beginning of Jesus' ministry took place in a new area away from his home town of Nazareth.

My own journey has not so much seen me enter a new land in its physical sense, but at every significant stage in my healing. I have felt internally and spiritually that I've entered a new land and arrived in a new place.

There has been a common pattern in the process of entering a new land. I initially experienced a feeling of such peace and elation. The shift has often taken place unknowingly but coincides with something significant that happened. Inside, there is often a feeling of such joy that I've arrived somewhere new. I sit and look around in this new place and work out where I've arrived.

I then begin to realise that my eyes see differently. What had previously seemed impossible suddenly has new hope and seems possible! And then a fragility comes, an overwhelming feeling and I wobble. I wobble like Peter who stepped out of the boat and onto the water in great elation of his belief in the miracle of Jesus. After the elation and his new belief and insight came the wobble. There is something in our human nature perhaps that prevents us from being able to completely step out on the water. Jesus knows that.

As I step out into the new place it's as if I've been unravelled. There is an image of Mary Magdalene going into the open tomb where Jesus had been buried and finding the linen cloths unravelled that had once bound Jesus in his death. His risen life had freed him from those cloths and ultimately he returned in all fullness to his father. To rise to new life in God is to be free from all that has bound us. All that binds me shall not be completely unravelled until

I return to God, but as I take another step along the way, another layer of cloths unravels.

And as another layer is unravelled from me in this life, I experience the human emotions of elation and vulnerability; and the spiritual process of being able to see and hear things a little differently. What was once impossible, through the grace of God, now seems possible.

The road to Damascus saw Saul's hatred for Jesus converted to Paul's absolute love of Jesus. His journey along that road saw his blindness unravelled into new sight. His old life shed, in fact physically shed from his eyes, as he walked with Jesus. Paul expressed his elation in the temples proclaiming the good news of Christ. But he also experienced vulnerability in knowing that he would endure persecution from some.

Our risen life will ultimately see us free from all that binds us, but each road we walk with Christ, each new land he leads us to, unravels us that little bit further.

Here I am Lord.

Amen x

Notes

Chapter 2

1. David F Ford, *The Shape Of Living* p147 (Fount/HarperCollins, London, 1997).
2. Joyce Rupp, *Praying Our Goodbyes* p38 (Ave Maria Press, Notre Dame, Indiana, 2009).

Chapter 3

3. Bessel Van Der Kolk, *The Body Keeps the Score* p10 (Penguin Random House, London, 2015).

Chapter 4

4. Rowan Williams, *Tokens of Trust* p viii (Canterbury Press Norwich, 2007).
5. *Les Miserables* by Victor Hugo. Words for the musical by Alain Boublin translated by Herbert Kretzmer.

Chapter 5

6. Richard Rhor with Mike Morrell *The Divine Dance* p116 (SPCK, London, 2016).

Chapter 6

7. Michael Mitton *Wild Beasts and Angels* p168 (Darton, Longman & Todd Ltd, London, 2000).

Chapter 9

8. Michael Mitton, *Wild Beasts and Angels* p39 (Darton, Longman & Todd Ltd, London, 2000)
9. Joyce Rupp, *Little Pieces of Light* p40 (Paulist Press, New York, 1984),

Organisations

a www.lifecentre.uk.com

Life Centre P.O. Box 58
Chichester.
PO19 8UD

Helpline 08088020808
Office 01243 786349

b www.crowhursthealing.org.uk

Crowhurst Christian Healing Centre
The Old Rectory
Forewood Lane
Crowhurst
Battle
East Sussex
TN33 9AD
Tel 01424 830204

c www.samaritans.org

The Samaritans.
Tel 116 123

d www.carolynspring.com

Carolyn Spring Ltd.
3 Archers Court
Huntington PE29 6XG

Tel. 014808 78687

Author Profile

Sarah J Chapman is a retired Anglican priest. She worked as an Occupational Therapist in mental health services for 18 years. After feeling called to full-time ministry she was ordained deacon in 1989 and priest in 1994 and then spent 15 years in parish ministry. Sarah began working alongside The Acorn Christian Healing Centre and spent part of her sabbatical in the USA with Revd Dr Russ Parker and Christian Healing Mission. In 2012 she became the Chaplain at The Living Well and Diocesan Adviser in Healing and Wholeness for the Diocese of Canterbury and was made a Canon in 2016. She retired to live in Portsmouth in 2019. Email revsarah@sargil.co.uk

Printed in Great Britain
by Amazon

67147857R00087